All In God's Time

Iverna Tompkins

Roxanne
932-8429

Mother Brunson
776-1395

Mone
410
3243

Aunt Joyce
484-4025

Darrol
432-0010

Leroy
630-0808

Janet
757-8758

CREATION HOUSE
BOOKS ABOUT SPIRIT-LED LIVING
ORLANDO, FLORIDA

Creation House
Strang Communications Company
600 Rinehart Road
Lake Mary, FL 32746
Fax: (407) 333-7100

Unless otherwise noted, all Scripture quotations
are from the King James Version of the Bible.

Scripture quotations marked NIV are from
the Holy Bible, New International Version.
Copyright © 1973, 1978, 1984, International
Bible Society. Used by permission.

To all who are seeking a fuller understanding of leadership anointing and especially to the students who first heard the contents of this book as lessons on the life of David.

Their eagerness to learn and willingness to lay aside preconceived ideas, coupled with a strong desire to be godly leaders, made the classes an absolute joy to teach.

Acknowledgments

Thanks to Carol Dunnigan for meticulously transcribing the tapes from the classes, to Liberty Savard who worked on the original drafts and to Shirlee Green who edited it page by page, and chapter by chapter, day after day.

Especially, I am deeply indebted to Maureen Eha who has been able to bring together in such a succinct way the many trains of thought and make a cohesive book rather than simply a Bible study. Thank God for her abilities.

Contents

Introduction

One of the most exciting revelations we can have as Christians is the understanding that God has a specific plan for us. The Scriptures tell us that God knew us before we were formed in our mothers' wombs and that He fashioned each one of us with a goal in mind. We are not mere accidents, afterthoughts or the results of a spark in our parents' eyes. We were created for a purpose!

Knowing that God has a purpose for our lives gives meaning to our existence, influences the choices we make and provides motivation for our Christian walks. But it can also cause us to become impatient whenever we seem to be doing things that are unrelated to our purposes.

Ultimately God's purpose for me was to be a preacher. But I was almost thirty years old before I began preaching regularly. In my younger days I was involved in the business world, social work and counseling. If I had known then what I would be doing today, I am sure I would have fussed and fretted about wasting my time. Now I can see that everything I have done has given me a much richer and broader background to understand and relate to people.

My time spent in social work and counseling, in particular, opened my eyes to let others know that without God we can do nothing. In my job, I saw people in bondage to sin of every nature. There were individuals involved in habitual sins, such as substance abuse or promiscuity, who genuinely wanted to change but had no power to do so on their own. I saw the futility of counseling that does not advocate conversion.

If you feel that you are wasting your time in getting on with God's purposes for your life, remember that Jesus spent thirty years learning a trade He would never use.

Esther was a concubine before she became a queen. And David started out tending sheep.

This book is actually the result of a question I asked the Lord about David's life. In studying the book of 1 Samuel, I noticed that David was anointed to be king of Israel when he was a young man. However, he spent the next fourteen years doing everything but ruling God's people.

"Lord," I asked, "why did You make David wait so long to become king?"

God responded, "Because I was making him ready."

This simple answer made me realize that even after we are called and anointed, we must be prepared for our roles in the kingdom before God can appoint us. Knowing our purposes does not automatically qualify us to fulfill it. The key to contentment during our periods of preparation is focusing on what God wants us to do while we're waiting.

If you have ever wondered when your road to royalty will end, then I believe this book will encourage you to prepare for the day of your coronation with patience and great joy. It will come, all in God's time.

Chapter 1

The Call

Picture this. You're standing at the end of a long line at the grocery store that is moving *very* slowly. You need to pick up the kids from school in ten minutes, so you begin to demonstrate your impatience in the hope that the line will move faster.

First, you sigh and shift your weight from one foot to the other, praying that the cashier will notice you're in a hurry. Next, you push up close to the person in front of you. Finally, you wave at the manager to indicate that he needs to open up another register.

"What is going on?" you ask yourself. "Is she waiting for a price check? Is she verifying coupons against purchases? Is she processing food stamps or a gift certificate?" All the while you're wondering and waiting and running out of virtue, you're thinking: "This is supposed to be the *express* lane!"

Most of us can identify with an anxious customer at the grocery store. But few of us recognize that we behave the same way in our spiritual lives. We have our purchases and our cash, and we want to get through the line as quickly as possible. We want God to take our money and send us right out with the goods for a hungry world.

Unfortunately, God does not always comply with our requests in a speedy manner. He is not moved by our impatience. He has His own plan and timetable for our lives. Why does He make us wait? Because He needs to make us ready to play our parts.

Each of us is called and chosen by God to play a specific role in bringing about His kingdom on earth. Second Timothy 1:9 says God has "called us with an holy calling, not according to our works, but according to his own purpose and grace."

Nowhere is this more apparent than in the life of David. When David was first called to become king over Israel, he had done very little to recommend himself for the position. He was a lowly shepherd boy. His only claim to fame was killing a lion and a bear single-handedly. Yet the call on his life to a royal post was unmistakable. At God's direction, he was anointed by the prophet Samuel while Saul was still on the throne.

Samuel himself didn't know what God was looking for in a king. When God instructed him to go to Bethlehem and anoint one of Jesse's sons as Saul's successor, he saw David's oldest brother Eliab first. Eliab was tall and handsome, and as soon as Samuel saw him, he thought, "Surely the Lord's anointed is before him" (1 Sam. 16:6).

But the Lord said to Samuel, "Look not on his countenance, or on the height of his stature; because I have refused him: for the Lord seeth not as man seeth; for man looketh on the outward appearance, but the Lord looketh on the heart" (1 Sam. 16:7).

David had six other brothers besides Eliab, all of whom appeared to be better qualified than a simple shepherd to rule over Israel. But they were left standing on the sidelines, while their youngest brother was exalted in their midst. Why? Why did God choose David over the other young men in his family? It was not because of what David had accomplished to that point in his life. He chose David because David had a heart of a servant, a willingness to do whatever God put before him to do, whether large or small.

The selection criterion has not changed since God commanded Samuel to anoint David as Saul's successor. It is still not outward appearance, but the condition of the heart and a view to His eternal plan that moves God to choose us for certain roles in His kingdom.

Nature of the Call

We need to broaden our understanding of what it means to be called. I believe that every Christian has a specific calling from God and a general calling from God. The general call is to follow God's guidance moment by moment. We were "created in Christ Jesus to do good works, which God prepared in advance for us to do" (Eph. 2:10, NIV). On the other hand, the specific calling is the particular role in God's plan that we must fulfill.

God revealed David's specific calling in an instant when Samuel anointed him to be king. However, when we look at someone such as Esther, we realize she spent years in the king's palace before she understood the purpose for which she was there.

David was called to be a king, but he was also called to obey his parents, tend sheep, take food to his brothers, fight Goliath, play the harp for Saul and so on. Esther was called to speak for her people on one fateful day, but she was also called to obey her uncle and live in a king's harem.

The call on David's life was not to attain a lofty position of leadership over God's people, but it was to serve God in whatever capacity God asked of him. David was faithful to this call, and, as a result, he became qualified for greater things.

We can think of a calling simply as an invitation to serve. From this perspective, our lives are one divine appointment after another. When God sets up an appointment for us, we need to respond wholeheartedly, never saying, "That's not my job." Anything God asks us to do, no matter how small or seemingly insignificant, it's our job to do it.

We don't need a clergyman's call, as

some think, to be effective. We need only to look around and let the Lord reveal why we are placed where we are at a particular moment.

Ultimately, if we seek God's direction moment by moment and follow it, we will find our specific callings. However, our lives are not "set on cruise control." There are alternate routes to the final destination, though God knows in advance what routes we will take. If we choose the more circuitous ones, He continues to support us, though His desire is to lead us along the easiest way we will come.

In my life, I have not always chosen the easiest way. In fact, I used to feel that I had started over many times by attempting one thing and then another. Seeing myself as failing whenever I changed jobs or vocations or places of residence, I would look back and think, "If only I had stuck with it or stayed there, I would have been thus and so."

Recently, I was contemplating this pattern and the Lord said, "Iverna, you have not started over in your lifetime." I was quite surprised, since I'd often spoken of the times I'd started over. The Lord went on to show me that in His perfect plan, my life was a continual journey. The detours I had taken by my own sin or stubbornness had not stopped me on this journey. They had extended it and made it more difficult, but God had never demanded that I start over. He had simply waited for me to turn back to Him and respond once again to His call.

Chapter 2

The Anointing

In charismatic circles, we often hear people speak of the anointing. They say things like, "Listen to him preach! He's so anointed!" or "Let's get in her prayer line. She's got an anointing for healing."

At times the word *anointing* is used almost casually, as if people were talking about hair color or personality traits. Other times it has great import, as if the person endowed with it is a divine messenger from God. Confusion about the use of this word today indicates that it is a term which is often misunderstood.

We need to see what the Scriptures say about anointing, both in the Old and New Testaments, and to understand how the anointing enables us in our callings.

Anointing in the Old Testament

In the days of Moses and the prophets, when the sacred anointing oil was applied to a person or thing, they were set apart for God's purposes.

God first instructed Moses to compound the sacred anointing oil when He was speaking to him on Mount Sinai (Ex. 30:23-24). This oil was used to anoint the tabernacle, its furnishings, the ark of the testimony, Aaron and his sons (Ex. 30:26-30). Later, the sacred oil was used by the prophets to anoint kings like Saul and David (1 Sam. 10:1; 16:13). The anointing oil was poured over their heads.

It is easy to understand why God chose oil as a symbol of consecration; it was an element His people could relate to. Even common oil was precious to the Israelites and was used in a variety of ways as an integral part of their lives.

- Oil was used to give light (Ex. 25:6; 27:20; 39:37; Matt. 25:3).
- Oil was used for provision (1 Kin. 17:12).

- Oil was used for healing (Is. 1:6; Mark 6:13; Luke 10:34; James 5:14).
- Oil was used for beautifying, perfuming and protecting the skin (Esth. 2:12; Ps. 104:15; Eccl. 9:8).
- Oil was used to prevent sympathy in times of fasting (Matt 6:17).
- Oil was used as a symbol of joy (Ps. 45:7; Is. 61:3; Heb. 1:9).
- Oil was used as an act of worship (Gen. 28:18; 35:14).
- Oil was used as a tithe, an offering to the Lord (Deut. 14:23).

In a spiritual sense, the Holy Spirit is both our sacred and our common oil today. He anoints us to serve God, but He also brings light, provision, beauty and healing to our lives. He takes away our need for sympathy, crowns us with joy, leads us into worship and sanctifies our offerings.

Anointing in the New Testament

Under the new covenant, our anointing does not come from having oil poured over heads in a literal way. Our anointing comes from the presence of the Holy Spirit in our hearts.

Jesus said, "It is expedient for you that I go away" (John 16:7). Only after Jesus returned to the Father could that portion of God which provides the enabling power — His Spirit — come into you and me.

Jesus told His disciples that they would be baptized in the Holy Spirit. The word *baptize* comes from the Greek word *baptizo*. *Baptizo* means to take something and submerge it as you would submerge a piece of cloth into some dye.

When we've been *baptizo(ed),* old things — desires, habits and behaviors — pass away. Just like a cloth picking up color from a dye, when we are saturated with the anointing oil (the Holy Spirit) we resemble Him.

The purpose of the Holy Spirit's anointing is to set us apart into a relationship with the Father and to empower us to do whatever God calls us to do.

Jesus said, "But ye shall receive power, after that the Holy Ghost is come upon you: and ye shall be witnesses unto me...unto the uttermost part of the earth" (Acts 1:8). When we allow the Holy Spirit to come fully upon us, we become truly anointed to serve, capable of emerging into a life of power and influence for God.

Do you want to know where to go? Do you want to know what God wants from you? Then say to Him, "God, let me be

Your witness on earth. Help me to declare Your work until it is completed!"

The Anointing in Operation

One symbol of being *baptizo(ed)* is having the gift of speaking in tongues. You do not have to speak in tongues to be filled with the Holy Spirit, but you do have to be filled with the Holy Spirit to be able to speak in tongues.

Like Paul, I thank God that I speak in tongues (1 Cor. 14:18). When I don't know what to pray, I'm so grateful that the Holy Spirit is within me to pray what needs to be prayed. When I run out of words and I'm still longing to say something, I'm so glad that He is there to express in royal language what the King deserves to hear.

"But I just don't believe in tongues!" many protest. The only difference between the ability to speak in a known tongue and the enablement to speak in other tongues is that the Holy Spirit speaks all the languages of earth, past and present, and all the languages of heaven. To have Him within us, speaking unknown languages through us, is His way of saying, "See, I really am here within you. I did come with power, and I have baptized you with it." You'll never again doubt His presence once His power flows through you as expressed in the gift of tongues.

When the Holy Spirit baptizes us, He operates through us in other gifts besides the gift of tongues. We often speak of these gifts as "anointings." Outlined in 1 Corinthians 12:8-10, the gifts of the Holy Spirit include faith, healing, the working of miracles, prophecy, the discerning of spirits and so on. When a person says, "I am anointed for healing," or "I am anointed for prophecy," what they really mean is that they have allowed the Holy Spirit to work through them in a specific gift area.

At different times, I have had all of the gifts operate through me. If I were truly anointed for certain ones, then I would be able to use them at my discretion. But the Bible says that God gives them as He wills (1 Cor. 12:11), and He uses them where He wants to use them, through a submitted vessel. I am convinced that any gift of the Holy Spirit can flow through any Spirit-filled believer at any time, but only according to God's will and for the purpose of exalting Christ.

Sometimes a person may appear to have a greater anointing for a specific gift because his or her level of faith is higher for that gift. People will often extend their faith on behalf of the prophetic flow or the healing ministry, for example, to the exclusion of other manifestations of the Spirit. Or the Lord may appoint an individual to minister frequently in a particular gift. But we should be aware that if the Holy Spirit resides in us, He can function through us to touch people in any capacity that is needed, as long as our trust is in Him.

Daring to Be Different

The Holy Spirit in us gives us the courage to be different than those around us in the world, to step out in faith to apprehend that for which we were apprehended (Phil. 3:12).

We have been taught very little in our generation about being different. We have been discouraged from going against the general current or flying in the face of conventional wisdom. But everyone who ever did anything worthwhile in the Bible, including David, went against the mainstream.

The apostle Paul is a good example. Paul had studied under Gamaliel and was undoubtedly seen as a tremendous success in his day when he was persecuting the Christians. He was highly respected for his

24

legalistic righteousness and accepted in all social circles because of his lineage. But he found himself without friends after he was converted by his encounter with God on the road to Damascus.

In the days immediately following Paul's conversion, the disciples continued to fear him as they had when he was so bent on eradicating them. Because of his terrible reputation, there were no open doors for him to minister in the Christian arena. Yet, Paul was undaunted. He was faithful to his calling in spite of the lack of support and other obstacles he faced.

Making a Difference

With man, a majority is numerical; but with God majority is power: the power of the Holy Spirit. God never weighs out anything according to man's majority. One single soul dedicated to partnership with Him is all God needs to accomplish anything He wants.

We humans often think that big groups will impress others simply because of their size.

For example, I remember leading the first Washington for Jesus march as the women's coordinator. We took two hundred fifty thousand people to Washington, D.C., hoping to be noticed. "Look at *all* of us Christians!" we said. We thought our numerical majority would cause congressmen to jump out of their seats and say, "Wow! I didn't know there were that many!" But with all of our thousands, the world just yawned and said, "So?" God doesn't need a big group to make a point or to demonstrate His power.

God's minimal requirements notwithstanding, one can be a lonely number, especially when society at large is asking, "Who do you think you are? You can't make any difference." There are times that I am tempted to believe this accusation. I get very weary and find myself wondering, "What difference *has* my struggling to swim upstream made?" Who hasn't looked back on their endeavors and felt that they looked more like mud puddles than a mighty, flowing river?

But then God says, "Wait a minute. If just one of you connects with Me and My will, a thousand evil spirits can be put to flight!" (see Deut. 32:30; Josh. 23:10) Think of a thousand devils from hell being blasted out of a community when just one anointed Christian connects with God. Think what happens when two people connect! It's not just two thousand put to flight; it's ten thousand!

Our ability to effectively "connect" with God is dependent on our being in the right place at the right time. Proverbs 18:10 says, "A man's gift maketh room for him and bringeth him before great men." In secular terms, Solomon was speaking of the power of a bribe, but the principle also applies to spiritual matters. Our gift (the Holy Spirit) will make a place for us anywhere and anytime God wants us to go. The anointing will put us before anyone God wants us to see. Only the gift of God's anointing within us, through the indwelling of the Holy Spirit, will ever open these kinds of doors.

Summary

David's story began with his call and his anointing, just as ours does. David's specific calling was to be a king, and some of us know our specific callings as well. But others are more like Esther, seeking God's guidance day by day, but not yet seeing the big picture. In either case, representing God on earth requires a call and an anointing. The call is our invitation to serve. The anointing is our empowerment to serve. Both are readily available to anyone who is in Christ. However, we need keys to release the work of the Holy Spirit in our lives. We'll look at these in the next chapter.

Chapter 3

The Release of the Holy Spirit

When I was young in ministry, a father of the faith invited me to speak to his church. Before the service, he prayed, "Let the anointing rise."

I was surprised. I had always heard people pray, "Let the anointing fall. O Lord, let it come upon us!" For the anointing to rise was a revelation that has encouraged me ever since. It means that God is always "right there" within each of us. We don't have to pray the anointing down. We just have to get out of its way and let it rise from within!

The pure anointing flows forth from a human vessel to the degree that people allow their human natures to be crucified and taken out of the way. Sometimes people say to me, "Oh, there's a much heavier anointing on you this year than I have ever seen before." What they really mean is: "You've let less of yourself get in the way this year. There's more of Him getting through."

I don't have more anointing than I had before, but like David, when he finally took the throne, I have died to more of my nature and allowed God to develop more of His nature in me. I have been refined, like David was, while facing the untoward circumstances and challenges God has sent my way.

Let's look at what happened to David after his calling and anointing.

Now What Do I Do?

After Samuel anointed David, you would think that David would head off to the palace. But David went back out to the fields (see 1 Sam. 17:15). How wise of David to realize that if God anointed him, He would also appoint him! How wise of him not to push forward beyond God's time frame!

Many people have responded to an altar call, "If you'll just come down here tonight and offer everything in yourself to Him, God says He will send you to the world." They have gone forward, crying out, "Here I am, God. I'm ready to go." But after the service, God doesn't call them or send them, either one. Then what happens?

Unless there is maturity and trust within the believer, doubt comes. Perhaps frustration boils up from feeling trapped in situations of life. That's when people say things like: "I don't want to be married any more." "I don't want to be locked in here with these kids." "I want out of this dead-end job." "I'm ready now for bigger things."

When God doesn't seem to pick right up on the option they've offered to Him, some people think that if only they were disentangled from their responsibilities (marriage, children, job, school and so on), then He would let them go. That is a very dangerous thought to entertain!

It Takes Time to Be Developed

David waited nearly fifteen years from the time he was first anointed until he actually became king of Israel. But too many people try to move onto the throne when they're not yet qualified to rule.

I counseled a group of former drug addicts who got saved during the early days of the developing drug culture in our country. After coming off the street and accepting Jesus, they were anxious to go back and witness to their drug-addicted friends. I encouraged them to stay in the church and get strong in the Lord first, but they insisted that "God was calling them to go back."

They returned to the streets as witnesses, and, after giving their testimonies a time or two, they were dragged back into their former ways of life. They ended up broken and defeated. It was difficult, but they had to learn that God had not been in a hurry just because they were.

One missionary couple finished their academic training in a Bible school but refused staff training in a local church because they couldn't wait to get to the mission field. Several months after beginning their assignments, they became frustrated due to lack of finances and other pressures on the field. They came back home embarrassed and disillusioned.

They didn't go back to a local church where they could become adequately prepared. Instead, they dropped out of ministry altogether, declaring that they must not have had a call in the first place. Like the prodigal son, they demanded their inheritance before they were mature enough to handle it.

This couple is not an isolated example. I have seen many wonderful people who have not fulfilled their missionary callings because they didn't take the time to prepare before they went into the field.

I wish every person who is called would understand that they need to be taught how to build themselves up on their most holy faith (Jude 20), how to stay in the Word, how to overcome depression daily by reaching out and getting hold of God, and so on.

Maturity is the one necessary thing in our lives that cannot be instant. It takes day by day appropriation of truth to bring us into maturity.

The Furnace of Refining

When I first began my traveling ministry, I was frequently introduced to congregations by pastors who felt the need to apologize to the people for having a woman minister in the church.

They might say, jokingly, "For a woman, this lady is a pretty good preacher." Or quip, "If God can use a donkey, He can use a woman." Though I smiled publicly when I heard such preludes to my message, each off-handed comment was painful to me.

It was a long time before I realized that God was allowing these words to be spoken in my hearing to humble me. I'm not saying He wanted them spoken; I'm saying He wanted me to hear them.

Showing me how to deal with offense was one way that God chose to mature me. I believe God brings us to maturity by taking the situations in our lives and turning them into lessons, bringing us to humility, which is realizing that without Christ we are nothing but with Him we are unlimited in all our abilities and callings.

In those situations, maturity comes from staying on our knees, reading the Word, seeking the face of our Lord, keeping our mouths shut and tending the lambs the Father brings us until what is said or done to us *really* doesn't matter and our spirits have been subdued to meekness and self-control in all things.

Ability, Anointing and Authority

In addition to maturity, two other factors affect the outcome of anointing in our lives. These are ability and authority.

Ability refers to the natural capabilities

that God gives us. Authority refers to our placements in life. Sometimes these placements are God's plan and sometimes they come by human design.

From the chart on the next page, you can see what happens as authority, anointing and ability interact. Many people struggle in their Christian walks because they have not understood these three factors.

Here is a more detailed description of the situation shown on the chart:

Pride. We think that our natural abilities are sufficient to fulfill God's call and develop an "I can do it!" attitude.

Frustration (and insecurity). We are called and enabled, but have no place in which to function as God has called us to. We become insecure and begin to question our anointing because we have no authority to act.

Ignorance. We have a touch from God, but try to fulfill His call without studying the Word and walking in it.

Legalism. We have the freedom to act and the ability to function,

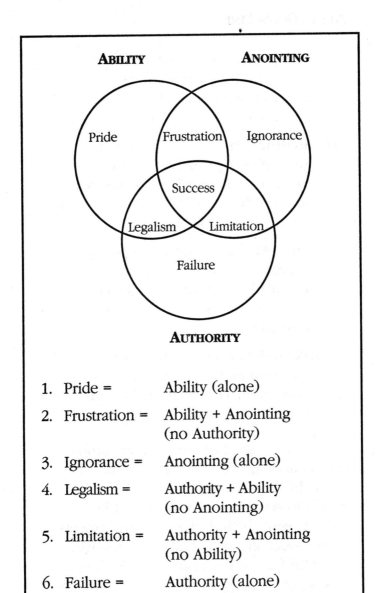

1. Pride =   Ability (alone)

2. Frustration =   Ability + Anointing
(no Authority)

3. Ignorance =   Anointing (alone)

4. Legalism =   Authority + Ability
(no Anointing)

5. Limitation =   Authority + Anointing
(no Ability)

6. Failure =   Authority (alone)

7. Success =   Authority + Ability
Anointing

but no grace and no understanding of the Bible's true intent. This position often engenders a need to control.

Limitation. We are limited in what we can do by our lack of ability; however, it is possible to develop ability when we have both the anointing and the authority.

Failure. We fail when we are put in charge of something that we are incapable of doing. We do not have the abilities to produce the desired results.

Success. When God calls, enables and positions, then we successfully fulfill His purpose for our lives.

It's easy to say that we need to combine ability, anointing and authority. But when we're living it out, sometimes it can be harder to see what is happening. When we are obedient to God, these three elements come together, and then we see sweet, beautiful fruit as the result. Let's look from God's perspective at one aspect of authority, our placement.

Chapter 4

God's Placements

During my younger years I worked as a supervisor in a county home for wayward girls. These girls were too delinquent to go into foster care, but not quite delinquent enough or old enough to go into prison.

The girls I worked with at the home were tough; many were gang members. But I always knew how to handle them, even when the other counselors, who were more educated than I, didn't. I adapted my behavior for every situation. At times I would slam the door when I entered a room, demanding attention, and other times I would be soft-spoken.

I would even go out after the girls when they would run away to rejoin their gangs. Sometimes these were very dangerous situations where these teenagers would be armed with guns, but I'd say with authority, "Come on home; it's time to go back." The girls would return with me.

Staff members would ask me, "How did you know what to do?" I would say, "You're not going to accept what I say, but the Lord showed me what to do."

My Christian friends thought, "She's right where God wants her." But I wasn't allowed to talk about the Lord with the girls, and deep down inside me was a sense that, "This is good, but it's not that for which I have been purposed."

I attended a special meeting at a local church one night and was surprised when the pastor confronted me. She put her hand on my chest, right over my heart, pushed me up against the wall and demanded, "Why are you wasting your life on things that are not eternal?"

At first I thought the Lord was telling me to leave my job. But the Holy Spirit quickly gave me God's answer to her question, "Because they have an eternal purpose." Although I did not see it at the time, something was taking place in me as I cared for those girls that was preparing me for a later time of ministry. I worked with the probation department for five years.

The Best Occupation

God uses placements to help us learn what He wants us to learn. Even when we do not understand why He makes us stay or why He moves us on, we can be assured that He is working all things for our good according to His eternal plan (Rom. 8:28).

One person who trusted the Father to place Him right where He wanted Him, uncomfortable as the situation might have been, was Jesus. The Scriptures tell us that Jesus learned obedience from what He suffered (Heb. 5:8). He could have called ten thousand angels to stop the Jews, the Roman soldiers, the high priest and Pilate when their actions were leading to His death. But He didn't because He had learned obedience through years of doing whatever God asked Him to do. Jesus recognized God's hand in His placement at every stage of His life.

Think back to when Jesus was twelve years old and His parents were returning home from the city of Jerusalem, unaware that He had stayed behind (Luke 2:43).

Oblivious to His parents' absence and their concern for Him, Jesus was having a wonderful time in the temple with the elders, who marvelled over His understanding. He might have been thinking something like this: "Finally, I'm free to be and do what I came to be and do. Yes! It is time for the teaching, the healing and the miracles!"

Then His mother showed up. The same God who had been giving Him amazing answers to the elders' questions, silently told Him, "Go with Your mother." Don't you think Jesus was just a little disappointed?

Now consider what we know about Jesus' life after the incident in Jerusalem up until the beginning of His formal ministry. Because all Jewish sons learned the trades of their fathers, we know that Jesus spent His early years learning to become a carpenter. I think He must have thought at least once, "Why am I learning this? Why am I here at home right now instead of out there with the people? I have so little time." Yet He submitted to God's plan.

From God's perspective, it isn't our occupations that matter; it's what we're learning that counts. He says, "Are you learning love, joy, peace, patience, kindness, goodness, faith, gentleness and self-control? Great! If not, I'll move you to a more intense placement where you will."

Some of us will be led to get advanced college degrees. Some will be led to be teachers, mechanics, construction workers, accountants, secretaries and so on. Will we use our degrees or our job skills in eternity? I don't know, but I know these things open doors for us to accomplish the purposes of God on earth.

Sometimes we say to God, in effect, "Lord, I trust You, but it would certainly help if You'd tell me why I'm here. Please just explain what You're doing, why, when and how much it will cost." But God has little sympathy for our desire to know His plans in advance. He replies, "That isn't the way I work. That's the way man works."

Many have a great anointing on their lives and receive prophetic utterances about the nature of their calls, but they do not live so as to fulfill the prophetic words. I am frustrated with them, but the delay does not frustrate God. God knows they are not ready, so He just keeps moving them from placement to placement to help them grow.

Difficult Placements

Let's look at the way God used placements in David's life to develop character in him.

In biblical times, there weren't too many placements more humble than that of a shepherd. Keeping the sheep was the least desirable of all chores in a family, and it was considered a dishonor to be consigned to it.

We have a tendency to romanticize Old Testament shepherding, thinking it was all pastoral scenes and peaceful beauty. But shepherding was not romantic or beautiful; it was demanding and monotonous. David had to protect the sheep from predators, keep them together, find food for them to eat, wait for them to finish, find water for them to drink, make them take turns and wait some more for them to finish. Then he had to get up the next morning and repeat the whole cycle all over again.

But David's experiences while protecting the sheep helped him to become brave, a characteristic he would need to face Goliath, the Philistines and other enemies. The periods he spent waiting on the sheep to eat and drink developed patience and gave him the opportunity to play the harp and fellowship with God, providing a skill and an anointing that he would need to minister to King Saul.

While David was still a shepherd, he was called to serve Saul as an armor bearer and a musician (1 Sam. 16:21,23). For a while, David had to divide his time between serving Saul and watching the animals (1 Sam. 17:15, NIV).

When David could not be with the flock himself, he "left the sheep with a keeper" (1 Sam. 17:20). After David killed Goliath, Saul "would let him go no more home to his father's house" (1 Sam. 18:2), and Jesse had to find a full-time replacement for his son.

Like David, we must care for the sheep God has already given us when He moves us from one pasture to another or from the pasture to the palace. We should do what we can to leave the sheep in the hands of a good keeper before we go where the Father sends us.

The greatest test for David was when he was rejected by Saul. When Saul became jealous of David, he determined to destroy him. David had to flee from the land of Israel. With his band of outcasts (1 Sam. 22:2), David moved from hiding place to hiding place, learning to trust God because he had nowhere else to turn.

Our rational minds would like to say that the reason David was not immediately made king was because Saul was still alive. However, God could have killed Saul in a instant if He wanted to. But because David still required much preparation for his placement, God left Saul on the throne and, in fact, used him to speed up the process of David's maturation.

God's Beginnings and Endings

The prophet Samuel was the first person to learn that God had removed Saul's authority to be king of Israel. First, God told Samuel, "Anoint Saul." Then God said, in essence, "Defrock him!"

Samuel was not happy about his assignment. In the same way, many of us are not happy about ending something God led us to begin. If God says, "Now start this," we rarely want to hear Him say, "Now stop it."

There are churches today that should not exist. Some of these churches were started under God's direction, but someone didn't listen when God later said, "Shut it down" or "Merge with another work" or "Go in a new direction."

This happened at a church where I had preached year after year. During one visit the pastor told me, "I feel that God wants my congregation to merge with a church across town. The pastor of that church feels the same." The plan was for both men to lead the new church because their strengths were complementary. We prayed together, and God confirmed the direction He wanted the pastors to take.

However, there was a group of people in my friend's church who didn't want to join the other church because they would have to leave their building. They insisted on staying where they were, hired another pastor and continued with business as usual, but the church never grew. Several years later it consisted of the same little group that had resisted following God's direction.

It is so easy to start out following God's placement but then go beyond it when we see success. I have seen several churches mistakenly come into being when God's directive was just to have neighbors in for coffee. God never mandated a new church to come forth; He simply called a small group to be hospitable and become more effective in the community.

We can find it difficult to believe that God would not want a successful home ministry to get bigger and become a new church. We find it especially hard when it is *our* successful home ministry.

At times we try to usurp God's role in reassigning individuals to new placements.

When a primary Sunday school class grows numerically and spiritually because there's an anointing on the teacher, we promptly give him or her more responsibility. If the same thing happens in the new placement, then we promote the individual again. The anointed primary teacher is promoted and pushed from position to position, until a level is reached where he or she is unable to function at all. Such people don't lose their anointing; they allow others to help them misplace it! They permit others to reassign their placement from God.

If we can learn that God's beginnings and endings don't have to make sense to us, then God can commit to us a lot of beginnings. He can rely on us not to mistake placement as a home group leader for a call to pastor a church. He can count on us not to promote people beyond the placement He ordained for them. He can depend on us to stop a work when He tells us to.

Accepting "Re"placement

At one point in his life when David was running from King Saul, he escaped to the cave of Adullam, where he was joined by his brothers and his father's household, as well as four hundred other men (1 Sam.

22:1-2). After arranging to leave his parents with the king of Moab, David set up camp in a "stronghold."

In this stronghold, David and his men were safe. His parents were secure in Moab. What was there to motivate him to ever move on?

When we get into a safe place (sometimes it's a church), we don't worry about the enemy coming from the north, south, east or west. We let the guards (church leaders) watch for us. If we have food (the pastor feeding the flock), water (the washing of the Word) and friends, we're really not inclined to allow God to change our placement at all.

I had a comfortable stronghold where I stayed for nine years — the wonderful church where my brother Judson Cornwall and I pastored together. I directed three choirs, the gifts flowed and we were very successful.

I liked being under Judson's protection. If people in the congregation had an objection to women ministers, I would send them to his office, and when he got through with them they had no more complaints. I loved living there, and I had no intention of ever moving.

Then God said, "I want to move you out

to the body of Christ." There was no way I was willing to hear that word. Everything was too wonderful right where I was, thank you. Then God spoke the same word to Judson: "I want you to go to the body of Christ." Judson, who was not stubborn like his sister, said, "Wonderful, Lord. Today or tomorrow?" And he started traveling, leaving me with the church.

I said to myself, "I can do this," and I pastored in his absence. I continued feeling comfortable there until Judson stayed away for longer and longer periods of time. He'd come home in the middle of the week and then he'd be gone again. Finally, it seemed that he was never at the church any more. God absolutely lifted him up and gave him a ministry to the body of Christ.

So I said, "OK, fine. I'll handle things here," and I began to dig in, but God rattled my nest good and hard. Through a series of events, I made a decision to resign from pastoring the church. But I felt unworthy to serve the Lord anywhere else.

Let me say something here about prophetic ministry. I believe that today, just as in the Old Testament, God uses prophets to confirm His Word to His people. However, false prophets can show up, too. This is why we must always let the word of prophecy be a word of confirmation or a word to be confirmed.

I was called out at one meeting and the prophet reiterated God's call, "The Lord's going to send you to the whole body of Christ." God had already spoken to me before I was called out in the meeting. With the pressure of God's previous words to me already bearing down on my stiff neck, I could no longer ignore the voice of God when the prophet repeated His message. I submitted to God's will.

David had a similar experience. When he was in his stronghold, God sent the prophet Gad to him. Gad told David, "Do not stay in the stronghold. Go into the land of Judah" (1 Sam. 22:5, NIV).

David had a lot of good reasons for not going to Judah. "They're going to kill me if I go there." "That's Saul's territory. I would be infringing on his rights." "I can't go to Judah until God makes me king." "I'm safe here."

Sometimes we really rattle on about why we can't do the will of the Lord. We act like it's OK to say no if we explain to Him why. Excuses or not, disobedience is disobedience.

Summary

Placement is something we have to deal with every moment of our lives. Remember: God uses placement to develop the fruit of the Spirit in our lives. These fruits will prepare us for future placements, so we must be willing to accept reassignment at times.

There is one placement that is permanent — our placement in our families. That's not to say that we've missed God if our families are less than perfect. As a single, divorced mother, I know what it means to struggle. But we can learn from the Word how we can fulfill our responsibilities to our families.

Chapter 5

Ministering at Home

Only a Christian mother with a prodigal child knows the stabbing — almost physical — pain that comes from watching your child throw away a godly inheritance on the so-called pleasures of the world. That's what I felt when my son, Dan, called me and said, "Mom, you're going to find this out sooner or later, so I might as well tell you. I spent last night in jail."

I thought, "My son! My son! My wonderful, good, God-loving, God-fearing son! What about all the years we went to church together? What about all the training I gave you in God's Word? I was shocked and devastated.

My son had been stopped by a policeman for having bald tires on his car, but he was taken to jail because the policeman found drugs in his pocket. He had gotten involved in the upper-class form of drug use — sniffing cocaine — that some of his business associates engaged in during their lunch breaks.

I thought I was going to die when I went to court with him. My heart ached so much that the pain is impossible to describe. My whole being felt like it was in the throes of childbirth. I told myself, "I can't live through this!" Yet I was trying to pray and be strong for Dan and not heap guilt on him for what he already knew was wrong.

Dan was released on probation, and I relaxed. I was certain that he had learned a lesson from his experience and thought that he would resist the temptation to resume his drug use. But I was wrong. He continued his sinful, but socially acceptable, way of life.

During this time, whenever I saw him, I felt like I was looking at a stranger. He was not my son. He didn't turn against me or stop loving me or even avoid me. But when he and his friends came over to visit, I would notice that their pupils were enlarged and that they were somewhat giddy and hyper. I knew that this was the reaction to drugs.

All I could really do to help my son was pray. "God, redeem him. Redeem him! He's Yours! I gave him to You when I was carrying him." For four tortuous years I had to hold on to my faith in God's Word, realizing as I did that it was God's grace rather than my training of him that would cause Dan to give up drugs and return to the Lord.

God responded to my faith and honored His Word by sending a Christian girl who was really on fire for God into Dan's life. Through her, the Holy Spirit brought Dan back to the Lord, and he gave up drugs completely.

Our First Mission Field

I firmly believe that our families are our first mission field. In fact, I'm convinced that the most important placement any of us will ever have is in our own homes. If we have unsaved loved ones near us, we don't need to worry about looking for our ministry; we already have it!

If you are a parent, your responsibility

starts with training your children. In China, small children are sent away from their parents for long periods of time for political and religious indoctrination. Little four-year olds who have had two years of training in Maoism will live in absolute conformity to that teaching. *HOME MINESTRY #1*

But in the church we are failing to train our children to hear from God. The attitude in our churches today seems to be, "Keep them entertained! Show them how to climb 'Sunshine Mountain' or play Bible baseball."

We don't spend enough time on spiritual training in the home, and we don't put a premium on raising up people in the church who will teach our children to hear from God. Children can hear directly from their heavenly Father just as adults can, and because they don't have our prejudices and preconceived ideas, they often prophesy more purely than adults do.

Young Samuel learned how to hear from God and prophesy His words at an early age. One night when he was living with Eli in the temple, Samuel was awakened by the sound of someone calling his name. Naturally, he thought it was Eli, so he ran to him and said, "Here am I; for thou calledst me" (1 Sam. 3:5). But Eli told him that he was mistaken and directed him to go lie down again.

Samuel heard someone call him two more times during the night, and both times he arose and went to Eli because "Samuel did not yet know the Lord, neither was the word of the Lord yet revealed unto him" (1 Sam. 3:7).

Finally, Eli realized what was happening. It took Eli a while to perceive that the Lord was calling Samuel because Eli was not accustomed to hearing God's voice, either. The Bible says that "the word of the Lord was precious in those days; there was no open vision" (1 Sam. 3:1).

Eli said to Samuel, "Go, lie down: and it shall be, if he call thee, that thou shalt say, Speak, Lord; for thy servant heareth" (1 Sam. 3:9).

When Samuel returned to his bed, he opened his ears to hear directly from the Lord. He was about to listen to the almighty God he had heard so much about — the very one he had been placed into the temple to serve but had yet to meet. The Lord called again, and Samuel answered as he had been instructed. God then spoke a fearful message to the child regarding the house of Eli.

When Samuel arose the next morning, he

was afraid to tell Eli the word he had received, but Eli insisted on hearing it. So "Samuel told him every whit, and hid nothing from him. And he [Eli] said, It is the Lord: let him do what seemeth him good" (1 Sam. 3:18). Eli knew that the Lord had indeed spoken.

Our children can be taught to hear directly from God just like Samuel did. When they are trained to recognize His voice, perhaps more of them will grow up like Samuel did. The Bible says of Samuel:

> And Samuel grew, and the Lord was with him, and did let none of his words fall to the ground. And all Israel from Dan even to Beer-sheba knew that Samuel was established to be a prophet of the Lord (1 Sam. 3:19-20).

Wouldn't we all like to see our children grow up with such an anointing?

I believe that today's young men and women are going to rise up in the faith of the Lord, recognizing God's voice and knowing they are perfectly kept in God's mighty hands. They will not try to be superstars, nor will they follow other superstars of the ministry. They will keep rank, being perfectly true to what God has positioned them to be, and they will move in power. God has said:

> And it shall come to pass afterward, that I will pour out my spirit upon all flesh; and your sons and your daughters shall prophesy, your old men shall dream dreams, your young men shall see visions (Joel 2:28).

Keeping Our Priorities Straight

We must be careful not to allow our relationships with Jesus and His body to become so intense that we neglect our relationships with our own family members. Otherwise we may sow the seeds of resentment in our unsaved loved ones. If we do not maintain our witness in a proper balance, those we love most will say, "He (she) spends every spare minute at the church — it's pretty obvious he (she) would rather be with those people than with me!"

It is never good to go out and do the work of the Lord if you must neglect your family to do so, especially if you are a woman. People will ask, "What have you done with your children (your lambs)?"

When David was sent to take food to his

brothers in the army, he left his sheep with a keeper (1 Sam. 17:20). David's eldest brother Eliab was quick to question him about it. He asked David, "Why camest thou down hither? And with whom hast thou left those few sheep in the wilderness?" (1 Sam. 17:28).

Eliab was still angry and resentful about David's anointing, so he questioned his brother's motive for leaving the sheep. In a similar way, people — especially people who feel they already have something against us — will question our dependability if we frequently leave our children with someone else.

I never traveled in ministry until my son was seventeen years old, and my daughter was married. My ministry was not my main focus when my kids were younger; my home front was.

I have asked my two children the question, "What do you feel you missed most in growing up?" They both answered, "We didn't know we missed anything." They felt this way because I always put them before my ministry.

There were two very valuable times for me to be with my children: when they got up in the morning and when they came home from school. Every afternoon before school let out I would leave the church where I was employed in order to get home and greet them when they came in. I would listen to them tell me about their day, talk over what they said, have a snack with them and then go back to work until supper time. It was as important for me to take care of the lambs in my home as it was to take of the sheep in the church.

Effects of Our Failure

The consequences of not ministering to our own family members can be far-reaching.

The Scriptures tell us that the sons of Eli "knew not the Lord" (1 Sam. 2:12). They habitually misappropriated meat from the sacrifices the people brought to be burned, and they "lay with the women that assembled at the door of the tabernacle" (1 Sam. 2:22). Though Eli rebuked them, they "hearkened not unto the voice of their father" (1 Sam. 2:25).

I have seen a similar pattern in some pastors' families. Sometimes their children are the worst behaved in the whole church. Because these kids have not been taught the value of a personal relationship with God and because there is so much pressure on them to conform, they rebel and do the opposite of what is expected of them.

Eli had a godly heritage. While the Israelites were still enslaved in Egypt, Eli's father had been chosen by God out of all the tribes of Israel to be a priest before the Lord (1 Sam. 2:27-28). God had intended for Eli's descendants to continue to minister before Him, but Eli didn't teach his sons to value God's call on their family.

"Why do you honor your sons more than me by fattening yourselves on the choice parts of every offering?" God asked Eli (1 Sam. 2:29, NIV). He held Eli responsible for their behavior and judged him harshly for his failure to train them properly. God told Eli through a prophet:

> There shall not be an old man in thine house...all the increase of thine house shall die in the flower of their age. And this shall be a sign unto thee, that shall come upon thy sons, on Hophni and Phinehas; in one day they shall die both of them (1 Sam. 2:31,33-34).

Samuel knew about God's judgement on Eli's family. That's the message that God spoke to him in the middle of the night (as we saw in the beginning of this chapter). But this knowledge did not prevent Samuel from making similar mistakes later with his own sons.

When Samuel made his sons Joel and Abiah judges over Israel, they turned aside after dishonest gain, accepting bribes and perverting justice, until finally the elders of Israel said to Samuel, "Behold, thou art old, and thy sons walk not in thy ways: now make us a king to judge us like all the nations" (1 Sam. 8:5). The wickedness of Samuel's sons had a direct effect on the Israelites' desire to have a king.

God's people still suffer when dedicated, anointed individuals place their sons, who are not anointed like the parents are, into their ministries. The sons cannot even sustain the ministries, let alone build on them, because God's anointing is not based on human heritage. Anointing is based only on our own spiritual understandings and personal relationships with God. A parent can lead his offspring to God, but he cannot pass down a calling or anointing to his children. God may choose a child to be the successor, but the parent cannot.

The stories of what happened to Eli and Samuel's sons are a serious warning to those of us who have children. Yet the Scriptures encourage us that if we "train up a child in the way he should go, when he is old, he will not depart from it" (Prov. 22:6). I believe part of our preparation to fulfill our callings must be establishing the life of Christ in our own homes.

Another facet of preparation that takes many people by surprise, although it shouldn't, is the trouble we experience when we are trying our best to stay in God's will. Have you ever thought to yourself, "Why do I have to go through this? Nothing good can come of this. This isn't fair." If you have, then we can identify with each other! I've said those words myself until the Lord showed me a higher purpose for my troubles.

Chapter 6

The Only Way
to Grow

Y ou are holding the church back."

"Women don't have the temperament to be leaders."

"What right do you have to lead this church?"

These were the words spoken to me dozens of times when I was pastoring a church with my brother Judson. People would visit the church on Sunday and then make an appointment on Monday to argue with me about what I was doing, even though I was submitted to Judson's authority.

Judson always told me, "Who cares what

they think?" But I cared too much. I started thinking, "They are right. I don't have any right to be a pastor. I'm divorced. I'm only here because my brother wants me."

Finally, several very respected leaders of the charismatic movement came and had lunch with me, saying, "God is using you here, but you are holding this church back because you're a woman and you're acting as the pastor."

At that, the last bit of courage left me. I resigned from the church, but the success that those leaders promised did not come. The church fell apart.

I tried going back to work in the secular world as an administrator and salesperson, but everything I tried just kept falling apart. Then I met a man who called himself a Christian and promised to help me. I trusted him with everything I had, but his promises were empty. In nine months I lost my home, my car, everything. All I had left were my two kids.

In that state of nothingness, the phone rang. It was a pastor and he said, "I understand you're available for meetings."

I just about dropped the phone. "I am?" I thought. I was so scared that I cried during the entire plane trip to the meeting. But God had been building character in me, and, to make a long story short, God put me back into the ministry.

Preparing Our Hearts

Truthfully, it is painful to write about some of the things God has brought me through, but I do it to encourage and prepare others.

I don't believe that God wanted those leaders to attack me or that it was His will for the church to fall apart. But I do believe that He wanted to build character in me, and He used those circumstances to do so.

It is wise to consider how we're going to react when we come to bring bread from the Father and we are faced with antagonism. We should never think we're so spiritual that we are immune to its effects. We need to prepare our hearts to reject the accusations that come our way so that, rather than being crushed, we are made stronger and more determined than ever to do God's will when the Lord says, "Here's the next loaf of bread."

Antagonism builds character. I wish someone had helped me understand this truth when I was younger! It would have saved me much anguish and a lot of anger toward those who were opposing me. I always felt I had done something wrong when I was broadsided with antagonism and my life seemed to go "boom!" in my face. No one ever told me that having to deal with antagonism was a great opportunity to grow spiritually. No one ever taught me to recognize the benefits of it so I could say, "Oh, praise God! There's a reason for this."

David dealt with antagonism when he went to deliver food to his brothers on the battlefield. His oldest brother Eliab accused him of being conceited and nosy (1 Sam. 17:28). David delivered the food in spite of it. Then he turned away from Eliab and looked to the battlefield. As a result, David killed the giant Goliath so "that all the earth may know that there is a God in Israel" (1 Sam. 17:46).

When we go to others, the only questions that we ever have to answer are: Have we been sent by the Father? and Do we have His bread? That's all! We don't have to question whether or not they will eat it. We don't have to be concerned about whether or not they approve of the person who brings it. That's none of our business, anyway. Have we been sent by Him and do we have His bread, period.

Once we deliver His bread, we must learn to do what David did: turn away from the accuser. Instead of becoming bitter,

David allowed antagonism to work "the peaceable fruit of righteousness" in him (Heb. 12:11). He then continued to seek to serve the Lord.

Character Is Grown, Not Given

God cannot give us spiritual maturity and strength of character through prayer alone. In other words, some character traits can be developed only through living out what we have learned is right to do.

We might pray, "Lord, I need You to give me patience right now!" But such a plea is useless. Patience is not given; patience is grown.

The Scriptures contain many object lessons which can help us to gain insight into the characters of the individuals described. As we read them, we need to ask, How can I learn from what happened to this person? How did he or she get into and out of certain situations? If we apply what we learn to our own lives, we will grow.

The life of David provides insight into some of the character traits God would have us develop. Listen to the testimony that one of Saul's servants gave about David:

> Behold, I have seen a son of Jesse
> the Bethlehemite, that is cunning
> in playing, and a mighty valiant
> man, and a man of war, and pru-
> dent in matters, and a comely
> person, and the Lord is with him
> (1 Sam. 16:18).

Let's look at the specific traits that were
praised.

1. Anointed Worshiper ("cunning in playing")

There were many qualified musicians in
the king's court, and any one of them
could have been chosen. Undoubtedly, the
servants saw a special something about
David's music. They may have thought it
was human talent, but as New Testament
believers we would identify that special
something as the anointing. The anointing
is what causes the Holy Spirit to touch our
spirits when certain individuals like David
lift their voices to sing and praise the Lord.

2. A Mighty, Valiant Man

The Hebrew meaning of the word
valiant is "personal bravery of heart."
David was mighty and valiant because he

had learned to trust God to fight his battles for him. His bravery of heart was based on his faith in the protection of the Almighty One.

When David offered to fight Goliath for the Israelites, he told Saul confidently, "The Lord that delivered me out of the paw of the lion, and out of the paw of the bear, he will deliver me out of the hand of this Philistine" (1 Sam. 17:37). And when David faced the giant on the battlefield with a slingshot in his hand, he fearlessly declared, "the battle is the Lord's, and he will give you into our hands" (1 Sam. 17:47).

3. A Man of War

David was in the habit of defending what he was responsible for. When wild animals took a lamb from his father's flock, he said, by his actions, "You're not getting my sheep!" He went out after them and delivered the lamb out of their mouths.

That's what we ought to say to the devil about our natural and spiritual families. "You're not getting my sheep: my family members, my church, my pastor. I'll fight for them!" Our battles take place in the spiritual realm as a result of our prayers.

> For we wrestle not against flesh and blood, but against principalities, against powers, against the rulers of the darkness of this world, against spiritual wickedness in high places (Eph. 6:12).

When you go off to war in your prayer closet, ask the Holy Spirit, "Where do You want me to focus my prayer today?" If you pray as He directs, He will deliver your lambs out of the mouth of the enemy.

4. Prudent in Matters

David handled practical affairs with wisdom, skill and good judgment. Let us order our lives prudently, as David did, so that we are above reproach. We should be so "clean" that we would not fear having the media walk unannounced into our homes, ministries or businesses at any time. We should be able to confidently say to any reporter, "You want to take a look around? No problem. Bring your cameras in? Sure. What would you like to know?"

I've heard Christian leaders complain when their applications for loans were denied. They cried "prejudice" or "persecution" when the banks turned them down. That isn't persecution; it's wisdom! Christians have earned the business world's suspicion. The church must come back to the reality of being accountable in practical matters as well as spiritual. We have to start addressing our own characters and quit railing at the shortcomings of non-Christians.

There are times when we'll do almost anything with sin except confess it. We'll deny it, rationalize it or explain it. Maybe we'll admit it just long enough to excuse it. "It's true, but here's why." It doesn't matter why! Sin is sin, and the only way to deal with it is to go to the Word and get cleansed. We read, God reveals, and we repent.

5. A Comely Person

Comely means "pleasing, graceful and honorable." David was "goodly to look to" (1 Sam. 16:12).

How do we, as Christians, look to the world? Societal standards for dress have dropped to record lows. People feel comfortable wearing all kinds of clothing in public, whether it provides sufficient coverage or not. Bathing suits have become common in the grocery store!

I think we Christians ought to be more careful to have a clean, modest look whenever we are around others. We also ought

71

to consistently maintain pleasing, graceful and honorable ways of expressing ourselves to those with whom we speak.

6. The Lord Is With Him

The Lord always shows Himself strong on the behalf of His people when they get out of His way. When we become more concerned about allowing Him to be seen than we are about what we want to express, people will be drawn to His anointing in us. They will approach us with questions they have never even acknowledged within themselves, recognizing that something is different about us and that we may have the answers to their needs.

Character Shines Through

Because of the character traits that Saul's servant saw in David, the servant recommended that David be called to serve Saul.

David's character made him the answer to Saul's need. That character had been built through his willingness to accept, deal with and finish whatever he was appointed to do. The Bible says that whatsoever our hands find to do, we are to do with all our might as to the Lord (Eccl. 9:10; Eph. 6:7). David was faithful to this command, both as a son and as a shepherd.

David went to Saul, and Saul loved him greatly (1 Sam. 16:21). Whenever David played the harp, the evil spirit that troubled Saul departed.

There was something very compelling about David, and I believe it was the Spirit of God shining through his physical presence. The same Spirit of God, shining unhindered through us, is the distinguishing characteristic of every single member of the body of Christ. We will draw others to us because Jesus is love.

Notice how David ministered to Saul. He did not condemn Saul for the presence of the evil spirit nor did he try to convict him. He simply ministered to Saul's need. Some Christians take pride in disturbing sinners' peace of mind when they come into their midst. This position is not the work of the Holy Spirit: it is pure human carnality. We are to be a blessing to others — believers and non-believers alike — by allowing peace, love and refreshing to flow through us.

The Character of a Servant

Each one of us has to settle this question within our own hearts: Do I want to be useful or do I want to be important?

If we are longing for recognition, God must limit our usefulness lest the glory associated with our positions destroy us.

Spiritually mature Christians do not worry about recognition. It is the novices (defined by level of maturity, not number of years saved) who are insecure about whether or not people know who they are. They want the world to know that they are God's chosen vessels.

What the world needs to know is that there is a Jesus! Not another preacher. Not another prophet. A Jesus Christ, Son of the living God, who was willing to die so they could live with Him eternally.

Will We Ever Be Done?

Recently, I prayed, "Lord, I'm so tired fighting myself. Every time I open up the Word, I see my own problems and shortcomings. Will the time ever come when I look in the Bible and see the words, 'Thou art finished'?"

As I prayed that night, the Lord spoke to me, "I know you get weary. Do you want Me to stop working in your life?"

"Goodness, no!" I responded in horror. I don't want Him to stop perfecting that which concerns me, even if it seems that it causes me to be in combat with my old nature every time I turn around. I want Him to keep on until He says I'm perfect.

Chapter 7

Warring to Win

One time I was attending a large meeting and a woman in the front row began to be disruptive, obviously under the influence of an evil spirit. When the interruption seemed to increase rather than decrease, the head of the meeting asked me to help.

Walking toward the front of the room, I began to pray, "Lord, how do You want to handle this?" There are a variety of ways to kick the devil out of a service. We can say, "In the name of Jesus, I command you to leave," for one. But this time, God's Spirit said, "Just get her to praise Me."

I said, "Let's all stand and praise the Lord." Several hundred people stood to their feet as I lifted my voice and said, "Praise the Lord, church. He is worthy to be praised!" We began to praise Him — really praise Him — deliberately ignoring what the woman was doing as we looked to Him.

As we continued praising the Lord in the meeting, I suddenly felt arms wrapped around me in a hug. It was the woman. Set free and made totally whole, this woman had stood to her feet and was hugging me, saying, "Oh, thank you, thank you!" Like Saul when David played the harp in his presence, she was released from the torment of the evil spirit through praise. When we get into the presence of the Lord through praise, evil spirits always depart from our immediate area of influence.

In that worship service, we faced one of Satan's demons directly. So what do we do when facing Satan directly and what should we do to overcome the flesh so that Satan does not even have access to us? Satan has a plan for our lives just as God does, and if we are to thwart it, we must know how to fight.

Confronting Direct Attacks

At times it is wiser to withdraw than to give the enemy the attention he craves. When David was in danger of losing his life at the end of Saul's javelin, he simply got out of throwing range (1 Sam. 18:11, NIV). When Jesus was about to be seized by the Jews and stoned to death, He "escaped out of their hand" and "went away again beyond Jordan" (John 10:39-40). On another occasion, Jesus "departed, and did hide himself from them" (John 12:36).

The key to being successful at warfare is this: Never stand up and fight when it's time to leave! The Lord is the one who assigns the battles, and the strategy is also His. We must come to Him and ask, "Which way do I handle this one right now?" He'll tell us.

God is so great, so mighty! He knows what's He's doing, even when we don't! If He wants us to scramble the devil's forces with praise, He'll tell us. If He wants us to command a spirit to leave by the authority of His name, He'll direct us accordingly. If He wants us to simply walk away, He'll make our strategy clear.

The point is this: When you are engaged in spiritual warfare, just obey what the Holy Spirit tells you to do and don't worry about the results or other people's expectations.

Recognize Satan's Strategy

We must ask ourselves, How have Satan and his demons managed to beat believers around as much as they have?

Satan often succeeds by isolating people before he attacks. We've made it possible for him to do this by refusing to come into one accord as the body of Christ (see Acts 2:1). We splinter our own spiritual powers with all of our denominational and doctrinal differences, making it easy for him to get a believer alone and accuse: "You Christian weakling, you don't really have any power. Look at the thought you had last night. Why, you don't even have a good testimony. People are never going to listen to you!"

Satan is the father of lies, but his lies are only damaging when he convinces someone to believe them. At the first whisper of deception, we should automatically grab our truth and beat him over the head with it.

What if Samuel had thought, "I don't have the proper lineage to be a prophet or a priest. The only reason I'm even working for God is because my mother abandoned me in the temple. I'm an unwanted orphan with no family of my own, a victim of my circumstances." Those facts may be correct, but they don't constitute the truth. The truth was that God appointed Samuel to be a prophet because that was God's plan for him. End of discussion!

We must stand on our truth and reject the flood of similar lies today. No matter what our circumstances, we are not accidents, and we are not victims! We're here on earth in this frame of time by divine appointment, and God intends for us to move in His power and bear fruit for His kingdom. Jesus said:

> You did not choose me, but I chose you to go and bear fruit — fruit that will last (John 15:16, NIV).

Deception in the Church

Praise should be Heard not silent

Another one of Satan's strategies is to get Christians to take a stand *against* godly truth! For example, a majority of Christians oppose praising God out loud in public or in private. I believe this is a deception of Satan.

Those of us in the minority must remember that people who do not understand the value of verbal praise are not automatically our enemies. Often they are believers who are simply ignorant of the glories of praising the Lord in this way.

We need to say to them, one on one, "I used to feel exactly the same way you do, that all this praise was a time consumer, that it was a ritual, that it was for show (or whatever you did believe). But I decided that if the Bible says to do it, I'd just do it. So I did, and it has changed my life."

We don't have to have a majority of people on our sides to change one person's concept of praise or any other godly activity which he dislikes. We will change hearts by sharing our testimonies, one-on-one. Don't ever forget that one and God always make a majority.

Opportunities for Satan's Attacks

Most of the time Satan attacks believers in their areas of weakness. He just seizes the opportunities individuals provide him by walking in sin.

Whenever there is hatred or jealousy in us, we open ourselves to evil spirits who delight in bringing injurious thoughts against others. God is Lord over all evil spirits and He will prevent them from harassing us when we do not give them an occasion. But if we are in sin, we actually create a passage for an evil spirit, as Saul

81

did by his jealousy of David. God only intervenes when we bring our lives in line with His Word.

Overcomers begin by overcoming their own sins. No matter who we are or what we have achieved for the kingdom of God, we must ask ourselves, Am I overcoming in myself? If we cannot say yes, then we must redirect our efforts. Our faith always grows when we triumph over our own failures.

Pray: "Lord, You're the Creator, and I thank You that I'm Yours. Please reveal to me the things that are keeping me from the fullness of Your promises for my life and for victory. Give me Your strength to defeat them."

Such a prayer is warfare of the strongest kind: war against the flesh! It is easiest to pray this kind of prayer when we're in church or in a serious prayer meeting and our flesh has been taken captive by the Holy Spirit. In that situation we will pray wisely because our spirits, not our flesh, are in control.

Nevertheless, the devil works overtime to undermine the work of the Spirit. He is a devious, underhanded opponent who knows where all of our weaknesses and hidden hurts are located and thinks nothing of using them against our good intentions.

We can resist him, as Jesus did when He was tempted, and he will leave us for a season (Luke 4:13). But we can't destroy him completely.

What we can do is kill the temptations Satan brings into our lives — *if* we want to. Often, we don't *want* to kill his temptations. We want to cage them up like pets so that we can take them out and play with them at times when we allow our carnal man to be in charge.

During these times, we remove the so-called pets — thoughts of hatred, revenge, sexual impurity and so on — from their cages in our old natures and fondle them, entertaining the thoughts with fleshly delight. Then, when we become aware of God's presence, we put the pets back into the cages and lock the doors.

We need to allow the Holy Spirit to open our eyes so that we can see the filthiness of these pets! Only then will we be repulsed enough to kill them. Only then will we throw away the keys and the cages. When He convicts us of our sin, it is time to say, "No more. It's over! I kill you right now." At that moment, God will support and sustain us by His power to overcome the flesh.

Focus on Winning the Battle

Satan does not fear a warrior, but he does fear a winner. The single reason for spiritual warfare is to win a spiritual battle. The subtle danger in spiritual warfare is that we become comfortable with being known only as warriors or, worse yet, worriers.

One of the diversionary tactics of Satan is to get us worrying in every direction until we lose our abilities to focus on winning the battle. A good soldier in a natural army does not say, "OK, I'll go out to the front lines and if I see this, I'll attack it. And if I see that, I'll get that, too. And, over there, I'll try to scatter them." When soldiers go to battle, they know what they're after and how to get it.

We need to stop worrying about warring in general and concentrate on winning each one of our battles in particular. We *will* win the war. That guarantee is at the end of the Bible.

What is the main battle in your home? An unsaved spouse or children? Rebellion? Compromise? All of the above? Ask the Holy Spirit to show you which battle to take on first and then stay with it until He releases you to go after the next battle. Once you are engaged, don't ignore the

84

other needs; continue to pray for God's intervention in all of them. But focus your study of the Word, your spiritual warring and your heaviest intercession to win one battle at a time.

Don't become distracted or derailed from following God's orders. Think of all the times you have determined to win a specific battle in your own life and instantly a crisis arose elsewhere that seemed to warrant your attention more. Distraction is a favorite diversionary tactic of the enemy. If the Holy Spirit has already given you battle orders, press in to carry them out and then wait for further direction. The other battles will still be there if He wants you to be the one who wins them.

We have touched on one of our most powerful weapons against Satan's power — praise. Now let's look more fully at praise and worship and their role in fulfilling God's purposes for our lives.

Chapter 8

The Perspective
of Praise

If praise weren't so powerful in the spiritual realms, Satan would not try so hard to keep us away from it!

For many years, every time I went to praise, Satan brought up my past to make me feel unworthy. Just about the time I would rise in praise, he would whisper in my thoughts, "You can't praise God. You didn't even make it in marriage."

In those years, divorce was a very big thing in my church. If you were a Sunday school teacher today and got a divorce, you were on the back row tomorrow. So

Satan used that to defeat me.

Then when my son wasn't serving the Lord, the enemy would add, "You didn't even make it work at home."

Satan is always the accuser of the brethren, and he always uses truth to tell his lies. The truth was that I had failed in marriage, and Dan was running from the Christian life. But that's not the whole truth. The whole truth is that I wouldn't deserve to worship even if I'd never failed. It's all grace. The Bible says, "Let us therefore come boldly unto the throne of grace, that we may obtain mercy, and find grace to help in time of need" (Heb. 4:16). When I grasped the whole truth, I was able to rise above the accusations of the enemy.

Satan still loves to haul out his big-screen TV and tell me, "Take a look at this, Iverna. Here is where you are. People are doing this and saying that, and now this is going to happen to you." I look at the ominous picture and thank God for teaching me through the years to just start walking to a higher place. I walk straight toward Satan's lie, and then I climb right up on top of it and shout with the psalmist, "I will bless the Lord at all times: his praise shall continually be in my mouth. My soul shall make her boast in the Lord" (Ps. 34:1-2).

Everything is so minute from that perspective; it's as though you've taken a ride in God's 747 and soared up to thirty-five thousand feet. Sometimes we need to climb up there and look back down at our troubles to say, "God forgive me; how dumb it was to get all worked up over those specks!"

David knew what to do when his feet starting sinking on this earth: he "rose up" by bowing down and acknowledging the royal lordship of his God through praise. Psalm 40 expresses his praise as a natural response to God's activity in his life:

> He [God] brought me up also out of an horrible pit, out of the miry clay, and set my feet upon a rock, and established my goings. And he hath put a new song in my mouth, even praise unto our God...Blessed is that man that maketh the Lord his trust. (vv. 2-4).

Beyond Praise to Worship

Many people use the terms *praise* and *worship* interchangeably. However, there is a clear distinction between the two. Praise is the doorway to the holy of holies; it is the entrance to worship. Worship comes when we enter into the holy of holies of God's presence. While the church has come a long way in expressing the worthiness of God, we often still stay in praise instead of entering into worship.

One case in point is the song of the Lord. The song of the Lord is simply the song that comes forth from our spirits when we worship spontaneously in His presence.

When the song of the Lord first came back to the church in my generation (though this was not a new thing as many assumed), it was so exciting. It changed our whole lives when the worship leader said, "Just sing unto the Lord, for He is worthy to be praised and together we shall exalt His holy name." Oh, the thrill of it that we could open our hearts and sing freely to Him out of our spirits! But we got so experienced at praising that it became quite possible to say all the right words about Him and yet never approach Him.

Praise may be offered outside the presence of the one being praised, but worship can be given only to one who is before us. I could say wonderful words of praise about you even if you were thousands of miles away, but I couldn't really adore you and worship you unless you were present with me.

It is the same with God. When I sing, "Great is the Lord, He is worthy to be praised," I am praising His name whether I am aware of His presence or not. But only when I behold Him do I cry from my heart, "You are so great, God! Oh, Lord, You are worthy to be praised!" because I know I am in His presence. It is then that I am worshiping Him.

When I'm singing, I often change references to the Lord to second person. Instead of saying, "He is worthy," I prefer to say, "You are worthy." It seems a shame not to pour out the wonderful words of the songs directly to Him. "You are Lord" conveys a whole different meaning than "He is Lord." The latter is a general expression of His place in the universe, whereas the former is a confession of His place in my heart.

At the beginning of prayer meetings and church services, we're often given the opportunity to stand and clap for the Lord. Our clapping is praise, but we wouldn't go up to God's face and clap in it! As we bring our praise directly to Him, saying, "You are my everything. You have done such great things," we enter into His presence and begin to worship Him.

One difference between praise and worship is that while praise fulfills our emotional need to respond to a holy God, it does not necessarily change us. Worship, on the other hand, does change us because we come face-to-face with God, beholding Him as in a mirror. Gazing at Him, we are "changed into the same image from glory to glory, even as by the Spirit of the Lord" (2 Cor. 3:18).

Understanding the awesome power of beholding God moves a church service beyond praise to worship, but it must be clear that praise is a necessary part of any service. That's because of the mixture of natural and spiritual that a congregation brings into any service. Praise enables us to make our transition from the natural into the spiritual realm.

Praise begins when I say to my soul, "Bless the Lord, soul. You will praise the Lord." I may not feel anything except obedience. It's still praise, because everything I'm saying about Him is true, but it is not worship. Praise is not worship until that praise is presented in person to the Person! Once we have come into His presence, worship can be either audible or silent.

In a service when the leaders don't know the difference between praise and worship, we often keep switching from one to the other. I was in a service recently that started off very much a worship service. Everything was God-centered and we sang several choruses. When we came to a song with the words, "You are awesome in this place, Mighty God," it reached an apex. In the recognition of the awesomeness of God, the whole congregation was drawn up into His presence. I was so thrilled. We worshiped and sang, and then the whole congregation went into the song of the Lord.

Suddenly the person who was in charge of worship changed the whole tempo of the music and began to sing an upbeat song called "Mighty Warrior" about preparing for battle. It was such a shock. I felt as if we all had to hurry up and go back downstairs because we had to go out to war.

As we switched tempos and sang that song, we praised, but we no longer in worshiped. When we're worshiping the Lord, we don't want to be drawn back into praise. When we're praising Him, we don't want to think about fighting the devil.

So is warfare wrong? No. Is praising wrong? No. Is worship wrong? No. But all of these things need to be orchestrated by the Holy Ghost so that we can move from the outer court into the holy of holies and respond in awe to Him.

Genuine Praise and Worship

Our praise and worship is born out of fearful reverence for God that is coupled with love. Fear of the Lord is not always accompanied by love, however; it may be coupled with hate. Fearful reverence, or awe of God, coupled with hate is the *modus operandi* of Satan.

Satan hates genuine praise and worship being given to God. He is constantly trying to spread his mix of awe with hate to anyone who will listen to him. That is why he has caused hatred, rebellion and messages of death to permeate the music of our youth. He wants them to think they are incapable of being touched by the hand of God but totally capable of destroying the works of God. By doing this, Satan tries to keep our youth from being channels for God's power.

Satan will attempt to draw you away from God's presence. He is extremely uncomfortable around anyone who praises and worships God. Satan is jealous, but more importantly, he knows the overcoming power of people whose reverence for the Lord is coupled with love. They are the ones who overcome their own flesh, the world and Satan!

Insincere Praise

Satan doesn't mind being around people who call themselves Christians, but never overcome anything. In fact, he loves to afflict them with a religious spirit. There is an "angel of light" side of Satan that delights in feigning worship through an unclean vessel, because he knows the vessel will remain untouched by God.

Backsliders who once had a relationship with the Lord can be found in churches everywhere with their heads held high and their hands raised, singing the same praise songs as everyone else. These people often deceive sincere Christians who believe that the sinners are there because they are repentant and seeking to be restored. In reality they may be fiercely stubborn in holding onto their sins as they stand there and sing worship songs.

What do we do when we identify someone who is offering insincere praise? It might be best if we do nothing. But if the Holy Spirit directs us to do something, it will be because the Holy Spirit in us identifies the unholy thing in our midst. Evil spirits, witches and demon-possessed people do attend church. In fact, these usually attend church on direct assignment by Satan.

The backsliders, on the other hand, are

94

Chapter 9

Inquiring of the Lord

I often receive phone calls from men and women who have a question for the Lord. They want me to pray about it and get the answer for them.

There was a time when I was younger that I would say, "I'll call you back." Then I'd spend hours in prayer getting answers for other people. I was carrying so many loads for so many people that I was exhausted and close to burnout.

One day the Lord directed me to the story in Jeremiah where Jeremiah spent ten days in prayer seeking an answer for the people of Israel. He came back to the people with his answer and they said, "No, we don't believe it" (see Jer. 42:1-43:2).

The Lord opened that Scripture to me. Jeremiah's heart was tender toward his people, but the truth was that he was wasting his time praying for their direction. The people were the ones who needed to spend the time in prayer. You see, in the process of seeking, the seeker is changed.

Now I tell most people, "I don't know what God wants you to do, but I'll pray with you that God will show you."

Choosing Our Battles

If we don't learn to inquire of the Lord, "Is this my battle?" the enemy will see that we are constantly fighting wars we were never meant to fight.

Too often, we justify our involvements by demanding, "Is there not a just cause?" I do not believe that a cause automatically constitutes a call. If I did, I probably would have died before I turned fifty. Why? Because I see causes everywhere I go.

The psalmist confessed, "Thou wilt show me the path of life" (Ps. 16:11). We need to inquire of the Lord as to where that path lies. I've learned that the real question isn't, Can I? The question is, Should I, God? You'll be surprised at how often the answer is no.

Before Saul entered into the first war with the Philistines, he went to Ahijah the priest and told him to bring the ark of God to him, the ark representing the presence of God. While Saul consulted with the priest, the Philistine camp became more and more confused. When Saul told the priest to stop the ceremony ("withdraw his hand"), Saul and his army went out to the battle and obtained the victory (see 1 Sam. 14:18-23).

But that was the last time Saul conferred with a spiritual authority before making a decision. God gave Saul many other victories in battles, but Saul battled on his own terms. Saul's self-reliance and arrogance led him to disobedience and rebellion against God, and God later rejected him (see 1 Sam. 14:36-15:29). Like so many of us who experience success at something and then decide we know how to do it from that point on, Saul stopped asking for God's guidance after his first victory.

There are many churches and ministries today that have risen with step-by-step directions from the Lord until they reached a place of success. Then their leaders stopped inquiring of the Lord. Surprisingly, when such churches begin to stagnate or go downhill, the leaders seem genuinely baffled. They don't understand that in ministry, as well as in marriages and individual lives, one thing is true: If you stop asking for God's guidance, you stop receiving it.

Capable Leadership

David learned to inquire of the Lord after experiencing several setbacks by relying on himself and others. By the time he left Adullam with his band of men and settled in Judah, he was in the habit of seeking God's direction before he made a move. So when the people told him that the Philistines were fighting against Keilah and robbing the food right off the threshing floors, he didn't rush off to the rescue, even though there was a cause. He asked God what he should do. God told him, "Go, and smite the Philistines, and save Keilah" (1 Sam. 23:2).

The only problem was that David's men didn't want to go. Although they were afraid that Saul would catch up to them and kill them, going out on the front lines against the Philistines sounded even less appealing. They protested, "Behold, we be afraid here in Judah: how much more then if we come to Keilah against the armies of the Philistines?" (1 Sam. 23:3).

David was not insensitive to the feelings

of his men, so he inquired again, and God replied a second time that he should go to war. Once David was assured that he was leading his men according to God's directive, he marched them off to the battlefield. The protests of the men no longer mattered. They didn't get a vote.

We need to be very careful that we do not lead people contrary to the direction the Lord indicates just because they vote differently. I try to make certain that I receive my instructions straight from God when those under the sphere of my influence ask, "Iverna, what shall we do?" I want to lead them in His steps and under His banner.

In some churches, people are frustrated because the leadership does not seem to have a directive from God. The leaders challenge their congregations according to their own ideas and ambitions. One week they challenge them to do this; the next week they challenge them to do that. Eventually the members of the church start leaving, and then new ones come in who get involved in this and that until they become frustrated, too. Haphazard, self-directed and unstable leadership demands a constant turnover of people for survival.

Proper leadership doesn't begin with good

ideas; it begins with inquiring of the Lord. A capable leader has to be the first to hear God say, "Here is My goal for this church." Then every individual in the church has to hear from God as to what part he or she should play in achieving the goal.

If you don't believe in the goal of your church, get on your knees and find out if you're in the wrong church or if you're just plain wrong. You won't do anybody a favor by being faithful and sticking it out if you don't believe in the direction the leadership feels God has said to go. The last thing a leader needs is people surrounding him who don't believe in the direction they are moving. I'd rather have a congregation of fifty who are unified in purpose than a flock of five thousand who aren't.

God Will Deliver Us

David took his men to Keilah and God gave them victory over the Philistines as He had promised. When we are willing to put ourselves on the line for God, He'll deliver us (see Ps. 18).

Saul found out that David was in Keilah and he pursued him there, knowing that the town was fortified in a way that would make it difficult for David to escape (1 Sam. 23:7-8). When David discovered that Saul "secretly practiced mischief against him;" he told Abiathar the priest to bring the ephod, so that he could inquire of the Lord about the intentions of the inhabitants of Keilah (1 Sam. 23:9). Would they protect him in return for his slaughter of the Philistines, or would they help Saul capture him?

David knew better than to expect the people of Keilah to support him, in spite of all that he had done for them. How many times have we been hurt because we put our trust in what we think people will do for us out of gratitude or respect, instead of asking the Lord about their intentions! God replied to David's question: The men of Keilah would deliver David over to Saul if they had the chance.

Once David had God's response, he and his men "arose and departed out of Keilah, and went whithersoever they could go" (1 Sam. 23:13). Eventually, they found strongholds in a mountain in the wilderness of Ziph, where Saul continued to seek them every day.

That same enemy who worked through Saul is still out to get the people of God every day. He is after us one way or another: fatigue, discouragement or distraction. But every day God delivers us when we are following His direction, just as He delivered David.

God continued to rescue David from Saul and his company over and over again. Even when the inhabitants of the land in which David sought refuge would tell Saul where he was hiding, God kept David safe. Saul did not understand that he was fighting a losing battle. He did not realize that he would never be able to hurt David because God was preserving him for a purpose.

We Do Not Have to Avenge Ourselves

At one point, David had the opportunity to kill Saul. While he and his men were staked out in a cave in the wilderness of En-gedi, Saul came into the cave to relieve himself. David's men encouraged David to take his revenge, reminding him that God had promised, "Behold, I will deliver thine enemy into thine hand, that thou mayest do to him as it shall seem good unto thee" (1 Sam. 24:4). But David refused to harm the king. Instead, he cut off the skirt of Saul's robe as proof of his advantage.

This was one time when David did not consult the Lord before he took action, and he immediately regretted his impetuousness. As soon as he had cut off the skirt of

Saul's robe, "[his] heart smote him" (1 Sam. 24:5). He called after Saul and explained that he had no intention of harming him.

After declaring his innocence, David went on to say, "The Lord judge between me and thee, and the Lord avenge me of thee: but mine hand shall not be upon thee" (1 Sam. 24:12).

If we had only one great truth from David, I believe it would be this: When we are following divine orders, we do not have to avenge ourselves. We do not have to follow up every rumor or lie and try to fight them. The Lord is our defense, and He will deliver us out of our enemies' hands. The apostle Paul said it like this:

> I know whom I have believed, and am persuaded that he is able to keep that which I have committed unto him against that day (2 Tim. 1:12).

God Will Sustain Us

Oh, how we need to have that same attitude today! "God, if You want to use me, You'll take care of me. You will keep me." Several years ago someone predicted there would be famine in America and Christians would be persecuted. Many people, including some friends of mine, took this prediction seriously and invested thousands of dollars in dehydrated food. They tried to get me interested in stockpiling it, too.

Had it been the Lord telling me to stockpile food, I surely would have done so. But I wasn't going to do it simply on the basis of my friends' recommendation.

I said, "I'll tell you my attitude. If God wants to use me during a period of famine and tribulation, then He can feed me."

We need to remember whose we are. We have forgotten our identity! We've rolled up our sleeves and taken care of ourselves for so long, we've forgotten that we belong to God. Our attitude is *"I'll* supply all my needs according to His riches and glory."

If we are so busy fighting battles that belong to the Lord, how are we going to fight the battles that belong to us? Remember, Satan would love to have us constantly fighting battles that are not meant for us. These battles may appear as innocent as good causes or as sinister as revenge. But if we will return to the habit of always inquiring of the Lord, we can learn to walk in constant victory.

Chapter 10

Ministering in Power

Early in my ministry I experienced what it was like to go into a ministry situation without anointing, and I hope it never happens to me again!

I was invited to speak at a certain church, and we had a glorious service. A pastor from another church in town was also at the service. He put pressure on the pastor I was visiting to let me go speak at his church on a certain night. Finally, the pastor I was visiting said OK. It was almost as if I had been sold for a night to the other church!

I didn't feel right about going, but I didn't know how to get out of it, so I went. When I got there, they took me to the pre-service prayer, which I normally love. When the elders stood around and laid hands on me, I heard myself praying, "Lord, I only receive from You. I only receive from You." There was some kind of wrong spirit that I sensed in *my* spirit.

When it was my time to speak, I had no anointing at all. It was just words, and I knew it was just words. I kept talking because I am a trained speaker and I can make words happen, but there was no flow of the Holy Spirit.

I had a friend in the meeting who had known me for years. He asked me after the meeting, "What happened to you?" I wanted to quit the ministry, I felt so badly about that night. Instead, I made a vow to the Lord that I will never again go under the pressure of men to speak. "Unless You send me," I told Him, "I don't want to go."

Natural Gifts

Do you know it is possible to minister without the anointing? I had no anointing when I preached at that church because I had gone without God's approval. Thankfully, I learned my lesson. However, there are too many Christian leaders today who know they have lost the anointing, but they continue ministering through their natural capabilities.

It is possible for us to be in a position of authority and to experience a measure of success in our endeavors without having the power and anointing of God. Saul is a biblical example of this. When the Holy Spirit departed from him, Saul ruled from his positional authority.

Saul turned to his natural gifts to sustain him. He had many followers. He had past victories which enhanced his reputation. He had the satisfaction of knowing that he had made it big from small beginnings, having come out of the little tribe of Benjamin. He had stature. He had the "look" of a king.

Undoubtedly there are Christians in places of great ministry today who, like Saul, do not understand the difference between their successes and the anointing of God. If they have favor with the right people, they mistakenly assume that they are where God wants them to be. But we must not be satisfied to go where people like us if God's Spirit does not accompany us.

Years ago, I began to pray, "Father, give me favor with whom You want me to have favor." I did this because I was having favor with wrong people who wanted to control my life and misdirect my energy. This is not uncommon in the ministry. When God uses us in a situation, we become the spiritual darlings of everyone involved — for at least twenty-four hours or so. The following week, we may not even cross their minds. If we allow ourselves to believe that we were special to them for any reason other than for what we could do, our feelings are going to be hurt.

Authority Too Soon

In the last charismatic move, many converts came out from sin, drugs and gangs, and too often we put them on a circuit to speak in front of hundreds, even thousands, of people. The reaction of the people to those testifying was to treat them as authorities on things about which they had no knowledge. As a result, some of the converts wrote books and became sought-after speakers, but many of them are not in any church today.

Were their testimonies real? The testimonies were absolutely real for the moment, but the people were put into positions they had no seasoning to handle. They should have been discipled in the process of growing into their usefulness. They should have been told, "Give your testimony and keep the focus on the One who delivered you. Now sit, be quiet and learn about this God who has brought You into His kingdom." Instead, we raised them up.

There is nothing wrong with new Christians being used to speak, but they shouldn't be given positions of authority within the body of Christ until they are prepared for leadership. First Timothy 3:6 says that we are not to put a novice into a position of authority, but some churches ignore the admonition in this verse.

Somewhere at the core of most problems in every church is a novice who has been placed into an official position he doesn't have the knowledge or anointing to handle. God does not want novices in leadership and authority in His churches because such placements can greatly harm them. They may be "lifted up with pride" and "fall into the condemnation of the devil" (1 Tim. 3:6).

Questioning God's Choice

Another possible reason for lacking power is because we question the appropriateness of God's call on our lives. Often we don't understand the criteria on which He bases

His choice, and we feel unqualified for the task He has set before us.

I have said many times, "Why me, God? Why didn't you use somebody who didn't have flaws in her background? Why did you pick a woman? You know how people hate women preachers!" Then one day the Lord really reprimanded me for my unwillingness to accept His appointment.

He said, "It's none of your business why I picked you, and I'm not getting rid of you." Just that quick. I didn't get any vote, and I hadn't volunteered either! The implication of this principle is quite simple: We don't get to vote ourselves in; therefore we cannot vote ourselves out.

A Broad Ministry

If we are to minister under the anointing of God, we must avoid limiting the scope of our ministries. Jesus said we would do even greater things than He did (John 14:12). But in order to fulfill this prophecy, we have to make ourselves available for a variety of tasks.

There are many reasons for the incredible success and blessing of the Father on whatever Jesus did, but one of them seems to elude the majority of the Christian world today. Jesus did whatever was necessary.

Where we lose it in ministry today is that we want to be specialists instead of anointed believers just doing whatever is necessary. Under God's direction, Jesus prophesied, preached, taught, prayed, healed, evangelized, discipled, shepherded and sent forth workers into the harvest. How could we possibly pinpoint a specialty in the scope of His all-encompassing ministry?

Many people put a cap on their ministries by naming their specialties and then never expecting to move beyond that sphere. We must refuse to place a ceiling on our usefulness to God! We also need to keep up our guards lest tradition or people box us into a one-dimension ministry.

When I first started traveling in ministry, the church was awakening to the masses of single people in congregations and the fact that leadership didn't know how to relate to them. So I was often called to hold singles' conferences.

Almost every television interview I had on PTL or CBN focused on talking about single life. Finally I got to the point where I said, "I'm not coming if it's going to be about singles." They'd reply, "No, we'll let you talk about anything." But when I got there, they'd steer the interview toward singles.

After a while, people just said, "Oh, yeah, Iverna Tompkins. She ministers to singles." The problem was God had not called me to singles ministry and I knew it. I started turning down invitations to singles conferences and little by little I got out from under the trap of being a specialist.

Sharing What God Has Given Us

One way in which we may limit the scope of our ministries is by restricting how much we share the revelation God has given us.

If only Saul had been able to see David in that same light. Saul felt so threatened by David's popularity, he plotted to kill him instead of sharing his knowledge with David. If he had poured into David what he knew about ruling, leading and warring, perhaps God would have poured out something new to Saul. It might even have been a greater understanding of, and a new relationship with, God Himself.

When those coming up in the ministry ask me for advice, I tell them everything I know. I don't hold select things back for my own knowledge and share only the less important tidbits with them. I pour into them whatever God has given me that would be appropriate to their ministries. I have shared dozens, maybe hundreds, of message notes and outlines. Ministers ask me, "Can I preach the message I just heard you preach?"

"Sure," I reply.

"Can I copy your notes?"

"Sure."

Usually they are surprised by my permission and frequently comment, "I never had anyone do this before."

Then I confess to them, "It's really not generosity. It's the most selfish thing I do. The minute I give my insight away to you, God is going to open something new to me."

If we minister in our own strength, we have to protect what we have done. But because everything we have comes from the Lord, we can give it away freely. That's the difference between ministering from our own capabilities and ministering by the power of the Holy Spirit.

Chapter 11

Trusting Our Source

When I first became known in the traveling ministry, some people said to me, "You are wasting yourself. You go out to minister, and even if there are only two hundred people, you pour out like there are thousands and then you get a paltry little offering. If you let us manage your ministry, you can speak just two nights a week and we will guarantee you a large honorarium."

They didn't talk only about money, either. They went on to say, "You will save your energy. You will last longer for the

Lord. You won't have to travel as much. You'll have opportunities you wouldn't have otherwise."

My flesh responded, "Yes! Where do I sign? When do I start?" But the Lord said, "You don't."

God said, "You may not minister that way. You belong to Me. I'll send you where I want to send you. I'll pay you what I want to pay you, and I'll protect you the way I want to protect you. I'll give you open doors that no man can shut."

He has done that, and is still doing it. He sends me to places I could never find on my own. I once went to a church that was shunned by surrounding churches in the area. The Holy Spirit spoke through me, and those poor, beat-up little sheep responded to the Word with such gratefulness that I almost cried! He knows where there are needs that I could never find.

No one can take care of and protect our ministries better than He who called us to it in the first place. When we are completely surrendered to Him, He will not allow anything to be done to us that won't ultimately bring us good.

Forming Wrong Covenants

One way we put our trust in others

instead of God is by forming a wrong covenant with someone. David fell into this trap when he made a covenant with Jonathan, Saul's son.

The occasion for the covenant was David's coming to live at the royal palace after David had slain Goliath. The reason for it was Jonathan's great love for David, which sprang up at their first meeting and probably was a response to the heavy anointing on David (1 Sam. 18:1).

Because Jonathan loved David "as his own soul," the two of them formed a pact (1 Sam. 18:3). Apart from the blood covenant, this was the strongest kind of pact in the Bible. To seal the pact, Jonathan gave David his robe, his garments, his sword, his bow and his belt. This was Jonathan's way of saying, "Everything I am and everything I have, I give to you."

The Bible does not encourage the making of vows or covenants with other people. We cannot be fully surrendered to God's will, whatever it may be, if we have submitted ourselves to someone else's.

The exception is the God-ordained covenant of marriage. God allows those who desire a mate to enter into the covenant of marriage, an agreement that says, "I hereby make a vow to bring my spirit, soul and body to you in this union." Such an agreement is strong and binding in God's eyes.

But relationship covenants are too strong to be made with anyone other than a husband or a wife. It is very wrong to make relationship covenants with a church or its leadership. Too many pastors have made pleas for their people to come into a covenant with them. Those of us who went through the whole discipleship and shepherding movement know the danger of these requests. Nearly every strong covenant group I've known has gone into error because of imbalance. If a pastor asks you to make a covenant with him, simply say, "I cannot join in covenant with you, but I do commit to you as my leader."

Divided Loyalties

The covenant that Jonathan made with David put Jonathan into an awkward position when his father later became jealous of David and wanted to kill him. Saul tried to make his son a party to the murder of the very man Jonathan had sworn to uphold, and Jonathan was instantly torn between two loyalties.

At first Jonathan tried to reconcile his father to his beloved friend. He "spake

good of David unto Saul his father" (1 Sam.
19:4), insisting that David had never done
anything wrong and reminding Saul of
David's bravery in fighting Goliath. Saul lis-
tened to his son and restored David to his
former position as personal musician and
deliverer, but the work of reconciliation did
not last.

As soon as the evil spirit came upon
Saul again, his anger was incited against
David and he tried to kill him. David fled,
but Saul pursued him, first to David's home
and then to Naioth in Ramah, where
Samuel and the other prophets were prais-
ing God. When Saul showed up in Ramah,
David fled a third time. Then David found
Jonathan and confronted him about his
father's behavior.

David demanded, "What is my sin before
thy father, that he seeketh my life?" (1 Sam.
20:1). Jonathan protested, saying that his
father was not plotting against David. But
David insisted, and Jonathan finally agreed
to determine his father's true intent toward
David and to let David know whether or
not he should run away.

David told Jonathan that he would hide
in a field instead of going in to dine with
Saul as usual. When Jonathan went to the
evening meal with his father, he would

tell Saul that David had asked to go to Bethlehem in order to attend a yearly sacrifice.

All the other times Saul had summoned him, David had obeyed and gone to the king in full faith that God would continue to go with him. But now David avoided Saul, because he had moved away from the presence of God and begun to assume the responsibility of protecting himself.

The covenant made between Jonathan and David became a stumbling block for David. David even began to lie, saying, "Tell your dad that I went home to offer a sacrifice." And Jonathan went right along with it.

Many people humbly begin a ministry and are anointed and used by God until they stop trusting Him to direct it. Usually they make this mistake because they are abused or misused in some way. Perhaps they minister and don't receive any payment for it. So they decide they need to change the way they handle their ministries. They send a letter to every group that requests their services explaining, "If I come to you, I expect this and this and this." Lots of ministries do that today and I know they lose out because of it.

Ministers of the Lord who place their

trust explicitly in Him and not in themselves find that for every place they've ever been cheated out of the offering God intended, there are many other places where the honorariums or offerings they received were far above what they ever hoped for or expected.

I ministered in one church where the honorarium was already prepared for me when the Lord spoke to the pastor and said, "Take an offering." He took an offering for my ministry, and it was much more than an honorarium. But the next place I go may provide less than I hope for or expect. The Lord keeps my accounts, not me!

When we measure our trust in the Lord by our circumstances, all the enemy has to do is to see to it that one circumstance turns against us, and our faith takes a hit and we begin to stagger. When we put all of our trust in the Lord, in spite of the circumstances, we may still be misused two or three times in a row, but our faith stays strong.

Extra Obligation

When Jonathan and David carried out their plan, it confirmed David's suspicions about King Saul. At first Saul was merely curious about David's absence from the meal, but he became enraged when he realized that Jonathan was covering for David.

Jonathan challenged his father, "Wherefore shall [David] be slain? What hath he done?" Furious, Saul grabbed a javelin and threw it at Jonathan, his own son, to kill him. It was now clear to Jonathan that his father would not stop until David was dead (1 Sam. 20:32-33).

Jonathan left and went out into the field at the time arranged with David and gave the signal that David should run for his life (1 Sam. 20:35-40). As soon as David saw the signal, he arose from his hiding place and he and Jonathan kissed one another and wept until David got control of himself (v. 41).

Before they said their final goodbyes, Jonathan reminded David that they had extended their covenant to include Jonathan's descendants, "Go in peace, forasmuch as we have sworn both of us in the name of the Lord, saying, The Lord be between me and thee, and between my seed and thy seed for ever" (v. 42).

Jonathan was saying, "Don't forget that we have this covenant relationship, David. You turned to me for help and I did what you asked." Many of us have felt trapped by people who have done much for us. Placing our faith in people and what they can do for us sets us up to owe them something back, but placing all of our faith in God is a very liberating and freeing relationship.

Destructive Dependency

If David had been functioning in the fullness of his anointing, he would have sought counsel from God's representative on earth: Samuel the priest. The only time we know that David went to Samuel was when he was in serious trouble. He ran to Samuel at Naioth in Ramah, where they were visited by the presence of God. In Ramah, David was at the place of God's deliverance, but he left that place to take counsel with Jonathan.

When we get too attached to one person, our judgment and our obedience to God all take a back seat to the human relationship. We can develop unhealthy dependencies on friends, spouses, pastors, leaders or ministries.

An example of the destructiveness of such a dependency can be found in some churches. If a leader becomes too revered and God moves him on, the church can fall apart. The person who comes in immediately following that leader doesn't have a chance, regardless of what he does. The Lord Himself couldn't please the congregation when they're distraught over losing the one who was so important to them! Usually, an interim pastor has to come and go before the people get desperate enough to relent and give up their attachment to the previous leader.

God does not intend for us to get so attached to our leaders that the work of the Lord suffers if He moves them on. I remember the first time a congregation developed a misplaced attachment to me. I went to a church where the people had been given practically no teaching at all. God allowed me to build this body up, and we had hundreds of young people coming in from the community. It was wonderful! Then I had to relocate and leave that church.

After three months, I had occasion to go back and visit. Right away I asked, "When is the youth service?" I was told that there was no youth service anymore. "But where did the young people go?" I cried. The response was, "Well, when you left, they quit coming."

The Lord showed me that I was never again to allow a ministry to be built around myself. We must never become that important to any person or group of people! If people are coming to church because they want to see us rather than because they want to worship and serve God, we know the fruit will not remain when we go. Jesus said:

> Ye have not chosen me, but I have chosen you, and ordained you, that ye should go and bring forth fruit, and that your fruit should remain (John 15:16).

We defeat God's purpose if the fruit of our work does not remain.

Repercussions of Sin

The worst part about David's self-reliance was that it had long-lasting repercussions, not only for David, but also for others.

After David left Jonathan, he went to Nob and found Ahimelech the priest. As David was at the temple, to his dismay he saw Doeg the Edomite, Saul's head shepherd. As a result, Saul confronted Ahimelech and accused him of helping David by inquiring of the Lord for him. The priest truthfully denied Saul's accusation, because all he had done was give David bread and Goliath's sword. He had never sought God's guidance for David, but Saul nevertheless ordered the death of Ahimelech and all his father's house (1 Sam. 22:7-20).

Doeg, the ungodly Edomite, carried out Saul's order to destroy the priests. In fact, he killed eighty-five of them. But he did not stop there. He went on a rampage through the entire city of Nob and killed "both men and women, children and sucklings, and oxen, and asses, and sheep, with the edge of the sword" (1 Sam. 22:19). Only Abiathar, the son of Ahimelech, escaped and fled after David.

When Abiathar told David what had happened to the priests, David was faced with the realization that his period of rebellion had brought about the destruction of many innocent people (1 Sam. 22:22).

When we are tempted to place our trust in someone or something other than God, we need to remember David's story. It may be hard to resist the temptation, but it is even harder — impossible, actually — to remove the effects of our sin once we fall. Just as David could not bring back the priests who had been slain, we cannot wipe out the pain our sins cause. The only thing we can do is repent and have faith that God will work all things together for good to them that love Him, as He has promised (Rom. 8:28).

Chapter 12

Letting Go

Most leaders, including myself, have given themselves as mentors to individuals that God brings into their lives. In the process of counseling these people over the years, we develop a deep affinity for them and take a personal interest in their spiritual progress. We want them to succeed, and we are excited to see them grow.

Samuel felt this way about Saul. Though initially Samuel had resisted anointing Saul because he knew God didn't want His people to have an earthly king, he grew to love him. Undoubtedly Samuel had poured out of himself into this young man, but Saul's disobedience created a troublesome situation for his mentor. It forced Samuel to choose between placating Saul and obeying God.

As mentioned in a previous chapter, Saul had been rejected by God because he disobeyed God's commandment to utterly destroy the Amalekites and everything that belonged to them. As a result, God told Samuel, "It repenteth me that I have set up Saul to be king: for he has turned back from following me, and hath not performed my commandments" (1 Sam. 15:11).

When Samuel heard God's response to Saul's disobedience, he was grieved and "cried unto the Lord all night" (1 Sam. 15:11). His reaction to Saul's unraveling position was an indication of the closeness of his relationship to Saul. Nevertheless, he went directly to Saul to tell him what the Lord had said.

Samuel began by asking Saul, "Hath the Lord as great delight in burnt offerings and sacrifices, as in obeying the voice of the Lord?" Then he declared, "Behold, to obey is better than sacrifice, and to hearken than the fat of rams. For rebellion is as the sin of witchcraft, and stubbornness is as iniquity and idolatry. Because thou hast rejected the word of the Lord, he hath also rejected thee from being king" (1 Sam. 15:22-23).

Saul begged Samuel to pardon his sin, but the prophet refused and turned to leave. As he did, Saul desperately reached out and grabbed the hem of the prophet's mantle and tore it.

"And Samuel said unto him, The Lord hath rent the kingdom of Israel from thee this day, and hath given it to a neighbour of thine, that is better than thou" (1 Sam. 15:28). He made it clear that God was not going to change His mind about His decision to dethrone Saul and anoint David.

Samuel left for Ramah and "came no more to see Saul until the day of [Saul's] death" (1 Sam. 15:35). But though he was physically removed from him, Samuel continued to mourn for Saul (1 Sam. 15:35). Finally God asked Samuel, "How long do you intend to grieve?" (see 1 Sam. 16:1).

I believe God is asking that same question of our generation. We have a whole generation mourning: We're mourning over our political leaders. We're mourning over the New Age invasion. We're mourning over the conditions of our cities. We're mourning over everything we see as negative in our society, from high crime rates to unrealistic taxes to sex education in the schools.

It is right to be concerned, to pray and to run for political office, but we change nothing when we just mourn. God is asking us: "How long are you going to mourn over what hasn't turned out the way you wanted it to?"

How long? is the question. How long will we mourn over what the Lord has said to reject? It might be a relationship, a job, an expectation or a position of authority. Whatever it is, if God has said, "Let go of that thing that's depleting your life," it is time to let go of it! Reject it or kill it, but let it go. So many things can become our "Sauls": things we have poured ourselves into because we wanted them to succeed.

God says to us, "You thought if you got the job you wanted, that would be it. You thought if you got the husband, the wife, the children, the house you were hoping for, everything would fall into place and your life would settle down. Your plan hasn't worked, has it? How long are you going to mourn over what I have rejected?"

When we respond to God's command and kill whatever is strangling us, He says, "Now that you have killed it, stop mourning it!" Generally, we want to continue grieving because we have invested so much of ourselves, and the mourning is the only tie we have left to what was so important to us. But if we do not cease mourning, we will not get new direction from Him. God never gives us new direction while we are continuing to live in regret of what we have just released.

Dealing With a Divorce

For many people, the thing they need to release is a failed marriage.

People who are divorced or separated and holding on in prayer for a spouse to return should keep believing — until the spouse remarries. Once that person is remarried, he or she is dead to their former spouse.

In my own life, I always hoped that some miraculous thing would happen in my ex-husband's life and that he would become the person I believed him to be when I married him. I kept waiting for that to happen, but it never did.

When my ex remarried, I had to say, "God, this is a part of my life that is not redeemed. For whatever reason, it is over, and he belongs to another now. I release him." But that wasn't all the releasing I needed to do.

I also had to release all the dreams, all the plans and all the things that I thought I would have because of my spouse. But until I released them, I couldn't go forward.

When We Let Go, God Can Move Us On

After God confronted Samuel about his mourning, He said to him, "Fill thine horn with oil, and go" (1 Sam. 16:1). And He sent Samuel off to anoint David, the future king.

Samuel didn't have any assurance that his next assignment would turn out better than the first one. In fact, when God told him what it was, he wasn't too sure he wanted to accept it. "How can I go?" he questioned Him. "If Saul hears about it, he will kill me" (see 1 Sam. 16:2). It was bad enough that Samuel had to tell Saul God was going to replace him; it was even worse that he would be the one to anoint Saul's successor.

But God wasn't accepting any excuses. "Take an heifer with thee, and say, I am come to sacrifice to the Lord. And call Jesse to the sacrifice, and I will shew thee what thou shalt do" (1 Sam. 16:2-3).

When we let go of our mourning, God will say to us, as He did to Samuel, "Fill your horn with oil and get on with your life. I'll tell you where to go and what to do." This is not an easy assignment. It

133

requires us to step out in faith without knowing why. It's especially hard if we have to call others to come and be a witness of whatever we may or may not mess up. We find it much easier if we know up front what God wants us to do later. Unfortunately for us, our knowing what comes next is not always a big factor on God's agenda. There really is no need for Him to tell us step two until we have taken step one.

For Samuel, step one was, "Quit mourning over Saul." Step two was, "Fill your horn with oil and go." Step three was, "I will show you what you are to do when you get there."

In order for Samuel to go forward he had to release the past. In order for us to go forward, we too must look to the future without any encumbrances from our past. May God teach us to hate what He hates, love what He loves, and release what He declares is over.

Chapter 13

Fear of the Lord

This entire book rests on an important assumption: that we desire to know God's calling for our lives and will obey it as it is revealed.

For this to be true in our lives, we must grasp hold a basic theme in Scripture: the fear of the Lord. When we stand in loving reverence of the Lord, we will order our lives according to His desires. The fear of the Lord will lead us to our purposes.

Obedience is the proof of the fear of the Lord, and, as David's psalms shows us, blessing is the result.

> O fear the Lord, ye his saints: for there is no want to them that fear him. The young lions do lack, and suffer hunger: but they that seek the Lord shall not want any good thing. Come, ye children, hearken unto me: I will teach you the fear of the Lord (Ps. 34:9-11).

Psalm 33 tells us that God's eye is on those who fear Him. He looks out for them, "to deliver their soul from death, and to keep them alive in famine" (v. 19). How grateful we can be for His protection and preservation! Nothing should frighten us more than to have God turn away from us and leave us to our own devices.

Psalm 112 gives a long list of blessings for the man that "feareth the Lord, that delighteth greatly in his commandments" (v. 1).

The children of God-fearing parents will be successful and blessed (Ps. 112:2). There may be periods of time during their lives when God allows the children to rebel and walk far from Him. But His promise of salvation and restoration for the children is not nullified by their rebellion. The fulfillment of it is only delayed for a season.

Those who fear God will have wealth and

riches (Ps. 112:3). Fear of the Lord and prosperity easily go hand in hand, because a God-fearing person can be trusted with riches.

They will have "light in the darkness" (Ps. 112:4). To us has come the light of dwelling in His presence, understanding His purpose and experiencing the grace of His provision. Thus we may fulfill the scriptural commands to "arise, shine" (Is. 60:1) and "let [our] light shine before men" (Matt. 5:16).

They will not be afraid of "evil tidings" because their trust is in the Lord (Ps. 112:7). We will know, as the psalmist proclaims, that troubles don't last for those who fear Him. If everything falls apart, we will declare, "He'll take care of us. He'll deliver us." We will always triumph over our enemies in the end, and our horns of dignity and authority will be lifted up (Ps. 112:8-9).

The Bible tells us, "The fear of the Lord is the beginning of wisdom" (Prov. 9:10). David walked in the fear of the Lord. In spite of the fact that he did some things he shouldn't have done, he always ended up turning back to God. God extends the same mercy to us. He doesn't tolerate deliberate sin, but He gently guides us to our purposes, despite the mistakes we make. Our roads through the wilderness will end at the throne, all in God's time.

About the Author

IVERNA TOMPKINS ministers full-time to believers of different denominations throughout the world. She is a gifted communicator known for her penetrating wit, uncompromising truth and concrete clarity. Her ministry is inspirational and prophetic, capturing the teaching of the Holy Spirit for the hour and bringing revelation from His heart to the body of Christ.

Through her writings, which include *The Ravished Heart* and *On the Ash Heap With No Answers*, she provokes readers to pursue the Lord in earnest. One-time founder and director of a training center for pastors and their spouses, Iverna has a long-standing interest in training for leadership. She currently resides in Scottsdale, Arizona.

Other Books by Iverna Tompkins

If It Please the King
(A study of Esther)

The Ravished Heart
(Lessons from the Song of Solomon)

On the Ash Heap With No Answers
(Based on the book of Job)

For a complete list of books and
tapes with information on the free
tape lending library, please contact:

Iverna Tompkins Ministries
P.O. Box 30427
Phoenix, AZ 85046
Phone: (602) 443-8001
Fax: (620) 443-8004

If you enjoyed *All in God's Time,* Creation House would like to recommend the following titles by women authors:

The Prophetic Romance
by Fuchsia Pickett

One of the most endearing love stories is found in the book of Ruth. Fuchsia Pickett's anointed insight shows how the book of Ruth is more than a love story, it also foreshadows Jesus as the Kinsman-redeemer of the church.

I'm Trying to Sit at His Feet, but Who's Going to Cook Dinner?
by Cathy Lechner

Do the demands of marriage, motherhood, finance and career seem never ending? In the face of life's pressure, many women pull away from God. Cathy Lechner shares her hilarious anecdotes and side-splitting stories. Her anointed words will minister life, hope and power to you.

Available at your local Christian bookstore or from:

Creation House
600 Rinehart Road
Lake Mary, FL 32746
(800) 283-8494